MASTERING SOCIAL MEDIA MARKETING 2023

The Essential Guide for Business Owners

Serkan PISKIN

Mastering Social Media Marketing 2023 - The Essential Guide for Business Owner, Copyright © by Serkan PISKIN

This book contains the necessary structural information for social media marketing.

With this book, where you can get up-to-date data and information for the year 2023, you can improve your business through social media.

All rights reserved. No part of this book may be used or reproduced in any manner whatsoever without writer permission of the publisher, except in the case of brief quantitaions embodied in critial articles or reviews.

index

Introduction	4
The Benefits	5
The Importance of Having a Clear Strategy	8
Developing Strategy	16
Settings Your Goals	23
Identifying Your Target Audience	28
Choose the Right Platform	32
Create a Content Plan	36
Budget	40
Resources	44
Integration with Other Marketing Efforts	50
Branding	55
Tone of Voice	60
Engagement	63
Collaboration	64
Social Media Marketing Tools	67
Employee Advocacy	78
Social Media Policies	81
Crisis Management	84
Timing	87
Repurposing Content	89
A/B Testing	94
User-Generated Content	100
Social Media Advertising	103
Influencer Marketing	109
Social Media Contests and Giveaways	115
Customer Service	118
Social Media Analytics	124
Social Media Monitoring	131
Social Media Automation	134
Social Media Guidelines	137

Introduction of Social Media Marketing

Social media marketing is the process of using social media platforms to promote a product, service, or brand. It involves creating and sharing content that is relevant to your target audience and engaging with them through various social media channels. The goal of social media marketing is to build brand awareness, drive traffic to your website, and ultimately generate leads and sales.

Social media marketing can be a powerful tool for businesses of all sizes. It allows you to reach a large and diverse audience, engage with them in real-time, and track the success of your campaigns through analytics and metrics. It also offers a range of paid advertising options, which can be highly targeted and cost-effective.

There are numerous social media platforms to choose from, each with its own unique features and demographics. Some of the most popular platforms for businesses include Facebook, Instagram, TikTok, YouTube, Twitter, LinkedIn, and Pinterest. It's important to carefully consider which platforms will be most effective for your business, based on your target audience and the type of content you plan to share.

To be successful with social media marketing, it's crucial to have a clear strategy and plan in place. This should include goals, target audience, content calendar, and a budget for paid advertising if applicable. Consistency and engagement are also key, as is staying up-to-date with the latest trends and best practices. By following these guidelines and being proactive, you can effectively use social media to grow your business and reach your marketing goals.

The Benefits of Social Media Marketing

Before diving into the specifics of social media marketing, it's important to understand the benefits that it offers for businesses.

First and foremost, social media platforms offer a cost-effective way to reach a large and potentially global audience. With billions of users around the world, you have the opportunity to connect with people from all walks of life and across a wide range of demographics.

In addition to reaching a large audience, social media marketing offers a range of other benefits for businesses.

These might include:

The cost-effective nature of social media marketing: Social media platforms offer a cost-effective way to reach a large and potentially global audience. This is especially valuable for small businesses or those operating on a tight budget.

The ability to reach a wide and diverse audience: With billions of users around the world, social media platforms offer the opportunity to connect with people from all walks of life and across a wide range of demographics.

The potential to increase brand awareness: By creating and sharing high-quality content on social media, you can increase awareness of your brand and what it stands for. By regularly engaging with your audience, you can build a loyal following and establish yourself as an authority in your industry.

The Benefits of Social Media Marketing

The potential to improve customer loyalty: Social media is a great platform for building customer loyalty and retaining your existing customer base. By creating and sharing content that engages your audience and provides value to them, you can improve customer satisfaction and strengthen your relationship with your audience.

The potential to drive traffic to your website: By creating and sharing content that is designed to drive traffic to your website, you can increase the number of visitors to your site and potentially drive more sales.

The ability to target specific audiences: Social media platforms offer a range of targeting options that allow you to reach specific audiences based on factors such as location, demographics, interests, and behaviors. This allows you to tailor your content and messaging to specific groups of people, increasing the chances that your content will be seen and engaged with.

The potential to generate leads and drive sales: By creating and sharing content that is designed to generate leads or drive sales, you can use social media to directly support your business goals. This might involve creating special offers or discounts that are only available through social media, or using paid advertising to target potential customers.

The opportunity to stay top-of-mind: You can stay top-of-mind with your audience and keep your brand at the forefront of their minds. This can lead to increased brand awareness and recall, and potentially more sales.

The Benefits of Social Media Marketing

The ability to establish thought leadership: By creating and sharing high-quality content on social media, you can establish yourself as an authority in your industry and build credibility with your audience. This can help to differentiate you from your competitors and increase trust and confidence in your brand.

There are many benefits of social media marketing for businesses. By understanding these benefits and developing a strategy that leverages them, you can effectively use social media to grow your business and reach your marketing objectives.

The Importance of Having a Clear Strategy

A well-defined social media marketing strategy helps to ensure that all of your efforts are focused and aligned with your business goals. It should outline the specific platforms you will use, the types of content you will create and share, and the tactics you will use to engage with your audience. Without a clear strategy, it can be difficult to measure the success of your efforts and make informed decisions about your social media marketing efforts.

Here are a few reasons why having a clear strategy is so important:

Focus:

A clear strategy helps to ensure that all of your social media marketing efforts are focused and aligned with your business goals. This can help you to avoid wasting time and resources on activities that don't contribute to your overall objectives.

For example, if one of your business goals is to increase brand awareness, then your social media marketing efforts should be focused on activities that will help you to achieve that goal, such as creating and sharing high-quality content that showcases your brand and sharing it on relevant platforms.

By focusing your efforts, you can ensure that you are making the most of your time and resources and that you are effectively working towards your business goals. This can help you to achieve better results and get a better return on investment from your social media marketing efforts.

The Importance of Having a Clear Strategy

Measurement:

"Measurement" refers to the process of tracking and analyzing the success of your efforts. This includes tracking metrics such as likes, comments, and shares, as well as more advanced metrics such as reach and engagement. By tracking these metrics, you can understand what types of content are most effective and make informed decisions about your social media marketing strategy.

Having a clear measurement plan in place is important because it helps you to understand what is and isn't working and make adjustments as needed. It also allows you to track the return on investment of your social media marketing efforts and understand the impact that they are having on your business.

There are a range of tools and analytics platforms available that can help you to track and measure your social media marketing efforts, including native analytics tools provided by the social media platforms themselves, as well as third-party tools such as Google Analytics and Hootsuite. By regularly tracking and analyzing your metrics, you can get a better understanding of your audience and the effectiveness of your efforts, and make informed decisions about your strategy moving forward.

The Importance of Having a Clear Strategy

Here are some additional details on the importance of measurement in social media marketing:

Understanding what is and isn't working: By tracking and analyzing your metrics, you can get a better understanding of what is and isn't working in your social media marketing efforts. This can help you to identify any areas that need improvement and make adjustments as needed. For example, if you notice that certain types of content perform better than others, you can focus more of your efforts on creating and sharing that type of content.

Making informed decisions: Measurement can help you to make informed decisions about your social media marketing strategy. For example, if you notice that a particular campaign is not performing as well as you had hoped, you can use this information to make changes and try a different approach. Similarly, if you notice that a particular platform or type of content is performing particularly well, you can allocate more of your resources towards those efforts.

Tracking return on investment: One of the main benefits of social media marketing is that it can be a highly cost-effective way to reach and engage with your audience. By tracking your metrics, you can understand the return on investment of your social media marketing efforts and see the impact that they are having on your business. This can help you to justify your social media marketing budget and make informed decisions about how to allocate your resources.

The Importance of Having a Clear Strategy

Understanding your audience: Measurement can also help you to get a better understanding of your audience and their behavior. For example, you can use analytics to understand the demographics of your followers, the types of content they engage with most, and the times of day when they are most active. This information can help you to create more targeted and effective campaigns in the future.

Overall, measurement is an important aspect of social media marketing because it helps you to understand what is and isn't working, make informed decisions, track your return on investment, and understand your audience. By regularly tracking and analyzing your metrics, you can get a better understanding of your audience and the effectiveness of your efforts, and make informed decisions about your strategy moving forward.

The Importance of Having a Clear Strategy

Consistency:

A clear strategy helps to ensure that your social media marketing efforts are consistent, which is important for building a strong and cohesive brand image. Consistency in your messaging, tone, and visual aesthetic can help to build trust and credibility with your audience.

This means that the content you create and share, as well as the tone and style of your communication, should be consistent with your brand identity and values.

Consistency is important because it helps to build trust and credibility with your audience. If your messaging and content are consistent, it's easier for your audience to understand what your brand stands for and what you offer. It also helps to create a cohesive brand image and ensures that your audience knows what to expect from your social media presence.

To achieve consistency in your social media marketing efforts, it's important to have a clear brand identity and style guide in place. This should outline the messaging, tone, and visual aesthetic that you want to convey through your social media marketing efforts. By following these guidelines and maintaining consistency in your content and messaging, you can effectively build a strong and cohesive brand image on social media.

The Importance of Having a Clear Strategy

Building trust and credibility: Consistency helps to build trust and credibility with your audience by clearly communicating your brand identity and values. If your messaging and content are consistent, it's easier for your audience to understand what your brand stands for and what you offer. This can help to build a strong and loyal relationship with your audience, which is important for driving long-term results.

Creating a cohesive brand image: Consistency also helps to create a cohesive brand image on social media. This includes everything from the colors and fonts you use to the tone and style of your communication. By maintaining consistency in these elements, you can create a strong and cohesive brand image that is easily recognizable and memorable to your audience.

Enhancing the user experience: Consistency in your social media marketing efforts can also enhance the user experience. For example, if your audience knows what to expect from your content and messaging, they are more likely to engage with your brand on a regular basis. This can help to build a loyal and engaged audience over time.

Simplifying your efforts: Maintaining consistency in your social media marketing efforts can also make it easier for you to manage your social media presence. By following clear guidelines and adhering to a consistent style and tone, you can streamline your efforts and make it easier to create and share content that is aligned with your brand identity.

The Importance of Having a Clear Strategy

Efficiency:

By having a clear strategy, you can more efficiently allocate your resources and prioritize your efforts. This can help you to get the most out of your social media marketing activities and achieve your goals more quickly and effectively.

Efficiency is important because it helps you to make the most of your time and resources and achieve your goals more quickly and effectively. By focusing your efforts and being strategic in your approach, you can get a better return on investment from your social media marketing efforts and achieve better results.

There are a few key ways to increase the efficiency of your social media marketing efforts:

Prioritizing your efforts: By focusing on the most important and impactful activities, you can ensure that you are maximizing the return on investment of your time and resources. This might include activities such as creating high-quality content, engaging with your audience, and running paid advertising campaigns.

Streamlining your processes: By streamlining your processes and automating tasks wherever possible, you can save time and reduce the risk of errors. For example, you might use tools to schedule and automate your social media posts or use analytics to track and measure your efforts.

The Importance of Having a Clear Strategy

Continuously optimizing your strategy: To ensure that you are getting the most out of your social media marketing efforts, it's important to continuously optimize your strategy based on the results you are seeing. This might include adjusting your content calendar, testing different types of content, or experimenting with different tactics to see what works best.

By focusing on efficiency in your social media marketing efforts, you can maximize the return on investment of your time and resources and achieve better results.

Developing Strategy

A social media marketing strategy should be tailored to the specific needs and goals of your business, and should take into account the target audience that you want to reach and engage with.

Developing a social media marketing strategy requires careful planning and consideration. By setting clear goals, identifying your target audience, choosing the right platforms, creating and sharing high-quality content, tracking and measuring your results, integrating with other marketing efforts, focusing on branding, tone of voice, engagement, collaboration, using social media tools and policies, considering timing, repurposing content, A/B testing, user-generated content, utilizing social media advertising, influencer marketing, contests and giveaways, customer service, and using social media analytics, monitoring, automation, and guidelines, you can create a successful social media marketing strategy that helps you achieve your business objectives.

To develop a detailed social media marketing strategy, you'll need to follow these steps:

Set clear goals: First and foremost, you'll need to determine your social media marketing goals. These might include increasing brand awareness, improving customer loyalty, driving website traffic and sales, or any other objectives that align with your business goals. It's important to set specific, measurable, achievable, relevant, and time-bound (SMART) goals to ensure that your strategy is focused and effective.

Developing Strategy

Identify your target audience: To effectively reach and engage with your audience, you'll need to understand who they are and what they are interested in. Conduct research, develop customer personas, and analyze your competitors to gather insights about your target audience. Consider factors such as demographics, interests, behaviors, and needs when identifying your target audience.

Choose the right platforms: Different social media platforms attract different types of users, and understanding which platforms your target audience is most active on can help you reach them more effectively. Consider the demographics, interests, and behaviors of your target audience when choosing which platforms to focus on. You may want to focus on just a few platforms that are particularly popular with your target audience, or you may want to use a wider range of platforms to reach a larger audience.

Create a content plan: Determine what types of content you want to create (e.g., blog posts, videos, infographics, etc.) and how you will share this content with your audience. Consider your audience's needs, interests, and preferences when developing your content plan. It's important to create a mix of different types of content to keep your audience engaged and interested.

Budget: Consider your budget when developing your social media marketing strategy. Depending on your goals and resources, you may need to allocate a certain amount of money towards advertising or other paid efforts to reach and engage with your target audience.

Developing Strategy

Resources: Determine what resources you have available to support your social media marketing efforts. This might include staff time, budget for tools or software, or access to other resources such as design assets or images.

Integration with other marketing efforts: It's important to integrate your social media marketing efforts with your overall marketing strategy to ensure that your efforts are consistent and effective. This might involve aligning your messaging and branding across channels, or integrating social media with email marketing or other efforts.

Consistency: Consistency is key when it comes to social media marketing. By maintaining a consistent presence and posting regular, high-quality content, you can build a strong relationship with your audience and establish your brand as a thought leader in your industry.

Branding: Make sure that your branding is consistent across all of your social media channels. This includes using the same logo, colors, and tone of voice across platforms. Consistent branding helps to establish your business as a trusted and professional brand in the minds of your target audience.

Tone of voice: Consider the tone of voice that you will use on social media. Will you be formal or informal? Will you use humor or be more serious? The tone of voice that you use should be consistent with your brand's overall tone of voice and should appeal to your target audience.

Developing Strategy

Engagement: Encourage engagement with your audience by asking questions, hosting polls, and responding to comments and messages. Engaging with your audience helps to build a strong relationship and encourages loyalty.

Collaboration: Consider collaborating with other businesses or influencers on social media to reach a larger audience and create buzz around your brand. Collaborations can be a valuable way to expand your reach and drive traffic to your social media channels.

Social media tools: There are many tools available that can help you manage and optimize your social media marketing efforts. These might include social media scheduling tools, analytics tools, and social listening tools. Consider which tools will be most helpful for your business and budget, and incorporate them into your social media marketing strategy.

Employee advocacy: Encourage your employees to share your content on their personal social media accounts. This can help to expand your reach and build trust with your audience.

Social media policies: It's important to establish clear guidelines for how employees should represent your business on social media. This might include guidelines for tone of voice, posting frequency, and types of content that are acceptable to share.

Developing Strategy

Crisis management: Have a plan in place for how to handle negative comments or reviews, or other crisis situations that may arise on social media. Responding promptly and professionally to negative feedback can help to mitigate any potential damage to your reputation.

Timing: Consider when you will post content on social media. Different times of day and days of the week may be more or less effective for reaching and engaging with your target audience. Use tools such as social media analytics to understand when your audience is most active, and plan your content accordingly.

Repurposing content: Consider how you can repurpose your content to get the most value out of it. For example, you might turn a blog post into a series of social media posts, or create an infographic based on data from a report. Repurposing content can help you save time and resources while still providing value to your audience.

A/B testing: Use A/B testing to understand which types of content and strategies are most effective for your business. This might involve testing different headlines, images, or calls to action to see which ones generate the most engagement.

User-generated content: Encourage your audience to share user-generated content related to your business, such as photos or reviews. This can help to build trust with your audience and encourage them to engage with your brand.

Developing Strategy

Social media advertising: Consider using paid social media advertising to reach and engage with your target audience. Advertising on social media platforms such as Facebook, Instagram, and LinkedIn can be an effective way to reach a larger audience and drive traffic to your website or other online properties.

Influencer marketing: Partner with influencers in your industry or target audience to promote your products or services. Influencer marketing can be an effective way to reach a larger audience and build credibility for your brand.

Social media contests and giveaways: Host social media contests or giveaways to encourage engagement and build excitement around your brand. Contests and giveaways can be an effective way to drive traffic to your social media channels and website.

Customer service: Use social media as a way to provide customer service and support to your audience. Respond promptly to comments and messages, and resolve any issues or concerns that your customers may have.

Social media analytics: Use tools such as social media analytics to track and measure the success of your social media marketing efforts. These tools can help you understand metrics such as likes, comments, shares, reach, and engagement, and can give you insights into what is and isn't working in your social media marketing efforts.

Developing Strategy

Social media monitoring: Use social media monitoring tools to keep track of mentions of your brand or industry on social media. This can help you identify any issues or concerns that your audience may have, and can give you the opportunity to respond and address them in a timely manner.

Social media automation: Consider using automation tools to help manage your social media marketing efforts. These tools can help you schedule posts, send automated responses to comments and messages, and perform other tasks to save you time and effort.

Social media guidelines: Develop clear guidelines for how your business will use social media. These guidelines should outline the types of content that are acceptable to post, the tone of voice that should be used, and any other rules or best practices that should be followed.

Settings Your Goals

Social media marketing goals are specific, measurable, achievable, relevant, and time-bound (SMART) objectives that a business aims to achieve through its social media marketing efforts. These goals might be related to brand awareness, website traffic, leads, sales, or any other specific business objectives.

Some common social media marketing goals might include:

Increasing brand reputation: By creating and sharing high-quality content and engaging with your audience, you can build a positive reputation for your brand on social media. This can help to attract new customers and build trust and credibility with your existing audience.

Increasing brand awareness: This might involve creating and sharing content that showcases your brand and its values, and building a following on social media platforms.

Generating leads: This might involve creating content that is designed to capture the attention of potential customers and drive them to take action, such as filling out a form or signing up for a newsletter.

Building customer loyalty: Social media is a great platform for building customer loyalty and retaining your existing customer base. You can achieve this by creating and sharing content that engages your audience and provides value to them, and by responding to customer inquiries and complaints in a timely and helpful manner.

Settings Your Goals

Improving customer satisfaction: By using social media to interact with your customers and address their concerns and questions, you can improve customer satisfaction and strengthen your relationship with your audience. This can lead to increased customer loyalty and positive word-of-mouth recommendations.

Expanding your reach: By creating and sharing content that resonates with your audience and using tactics such as social media advertising and influencer marketing, you can expand your reach and reach a wider audience on social media. This can help to increase brand awareness and drive more traffic to your website.

Driving traffic to your website: This might involve creating content that is designed to drive traffic to your website and using tactics such as social media advertising and influencer marketing to reach a wider audience.

Increasing sales: This might involve creating and promoting special offers or discounts through social media, or using paid advertising to target potential customers.

Settings Your Goals

How to work SMART?

Overall, setting SMART goals is an important aspect of any social media marketing strategy. By setting specific, measurable, achievable, relevant, and time-bound goals, you can ensure that you are working towards objectives that are aligned with your business objectives and that you can track your progress along the way.

Setting SMART: It's important to set SMART goals for your social media marketing efforts, which means that they should be specific, measurable, achievable, relevant, and time-bound. This helps to ensure that your goals are clear and achievable, and it makes it easier to track your progress and measure the success of your efforts.

Aligning goals with business objectives: Your social media marketing goals should be aligned with your overall business objectives. For example, if one of your business goals is to increase sales, then one of your social media marketing goals might be to drive traffic to your website or generate leads. By aligning your goals with your overall business objectives, you can ensure that your social media marketing efforts are contributing to the overall success of your business.

Specific: For example, instead of setting a goal to "increase brand awareness," you might set a goal to "increase brand awareness by 10% within the next 6 months through social media." This helps to make your goals clear and measurable, and it makes it easier to track your progress and determine whether or not you are meeting your targets.

Settings Your Goals

Tracking your progress: To understand whether or not you are meeting your social media marketing goals, it's important to track your progress regularly. This might involve tracking metrics such as likes, comments, and shares, as well as more advanced metrics such as reach and engagement.

Measurable: It's important to set goals that are measurable, so that you can track your progress and understand whether or not you are meeting your targets. This might involve setting goals related to metrics such as likes, comments, shares, reach, or engagement.

Achievable: It's important to set goals that are realistic and achievable, given your current resources and capabilities. Setting unrealistic goals can lead to disappointment and can discourage you from continuing to work towards your goals.

Relevant: Your social media marketing goals should be relevant to your business and its overall objectives. For example, if your business is focused on increasing sales, then generating leads or driving traffic to your website might be more relevant goals than increasing brand awareness.

Time-bound: It's important to set goals that have a specific timeline, so that you can track your progress and stay motivated. This might involve setting goals for a specific period of time, such as the next month or quarter, or setting a long-term goal with specific milestones along the way.

Settings Your Goals

Multiple goals: It's often helpful to set multiple social media marketing goals, as this allows you to focus on different aspects of your strategy and achieve a range of objectives. For example, you might set a goal to increase brand awareness, another goal to drive traffic to your website, and another goal to generate leads.

Long-term and short-term goals: It's important to set both long-term and short-term goals in your social media marketing strategy. Long-term goals are those that you aim to achieve over a longer period of time, such as increasing brand awareness or driving website traffic. Short-term goals are those that you aim to achieve in the short-term, such as generating leads or increasing sales. By setting both long-term and short-term goals, you can ensure that you are working towards both immediate and long-term objectives.

Reviewing and adjusting your goals: As you work towards your social media marketing goals, it's important to regularly review and adjust them as needed. This might involve adjusting your strategy, setting new goals, or revising your existing goals based on the results you are seeing. By regularly reviewing and adjusting your goals, you can ensure that you are staying on track and making progress towards your objectives.

Identifying Your Target Audience

Identifying your target audience is an important step in the process of developing a social media marketing strategy. Your target audience is the group of people that you want to reach and engage with through your social media efforts.

By understanding the demographics, interests, behaviors, pain points, and needs of your target audience, you can create and share content that resonates with them and is more likely to be engaged with.
This can help you effectively reach and engage with your audience, and achieve your social media marketing goals.

By conducting research, developing customer personas, analyzing your competitors, understanding the buyer's journey, using social listening, and integrating with other marketing efforts, you can gather valuable insights about your target audience and create a successful social media marketing strategy.

To identify your target audience, you'll need to consider a range of factors such as:

Demographics: Demographic information such as age, gender, location, and income can be helpful in identifying your target audience. For example, if you are selling a luxury product, you might target an audience with a higher income.

Identifying Your Target Audience

Interests and behaviors: Understanding the interests and behaviors of your target audience can help you create content that resonates with them and is more likely to be engaged with. For example, if you are selling outdoor gear, you might target an audience that is interested in outdoor activities.

Pain points and needs: Identifying the pain points and needs of your target audience can help you create content that addresses these issues and provides value to them. For example, if you are selling a product that helps people with insomnia, you might target an audience that is interested in improving their sleep.

Research: Conducting research can be a valuable way to learn more about your target audience. This might involve analyzing data from social media platforms, conducting surveys or focus groups, or using tools such as Google Analytics to gather insights about your website visitors.

Personas: Developing customer personas can be a helpful way to visualize and understand your target audience. A customer persona is a fictional character that represents a typical member of your target audience. By creating a persona, you can better understand the needs, motivations, and behaviors of your target audience and create content that resonates with them.

Identifying Your Target Audience

Buyer's journey: Understanding the buyer's journey, or the steps that a person goes through when making a purchase, can also be helpful in identifying your target audience. By understanding where your audience is in the buyer's journey, you can create content that meets their needs and supports them at each stage.

Competitor analysis: Analyzing the social media presence of your competitors can be a helpful way to gather insights about your target audience. You can use tools such as social media analytics to see which types of content are resonating with your competitors' audiences, and use this information to inform your own strategy.

Social media platforms: Different social media platforms attract different types of users, and understanding which platforms your target audience is most active on can help you reach them more effectively. For example, if your target audience is younger, you might focus more on platforms such as Instagram and TikTok. If your target audience is older, you might focus more on platforms such as Facebook and LinkedIn.

Social listening: Using tools such as social listening can help you gather insights about your target audience by tracking and analyzing social media conversations. This can help you understand what topics are of interest to your audience, and create content that addresses these topics and meets their needs.

Identifying Your Target Audience

Value proposition: Understanding the value proposition of your business, or the unique benefits that you offer to your customers, can help you identify your target audience. By understanding what sets your business apart from your competitors, you can create content that resonates with your target audience and highlights the value that you offer.

Customer feedback: Gathering customer feedback can be a valuable way to learn more about your target audience and their needs. By listening to your customers and gathering insights about their experiences, you can create content that addresses their needs and expectations, and improves their overall satisfaction with your business.

Integrating with other marketing efforts: Identifying your target audience should not be a standalone exercise. It's important to integrate your social media marketing efforts with your overall marketing strategy, and ensure that your target audience is consistent across all channels. By aligning your efforts, you can create a more cohesive and effective marketing strategy.

Choose the Right Platform

Social media platform selection is important because it can have a significant impact on the success of your social media marketing efforts. Choosing the right platforms can help you reach and engage with your target audience more effectively, while choosing the wrong platforms can lead to wasted time and resources.

There are a few key factors to consider when choosing the right social media platforms for your business:

Target audience: The most important factor to consider is your target audience. Which platforms are they most active on? For example, if you are targeting younger audiences, you might consider focusing on platforms such as Instagram or TikTok. If you are targeting business professionals, LinkedIn might be a better fit.

Business type: Different types of businesses may be more suited to certain platforms. For example, visual businesses such as fashion or design might be well-suited to platforms like Instagram or Pinterest, while businesses that rely on text-based content might do better on platforms such as Twitter or LinkedIn.

Competitors: Analyze your competitors' social media presence to understand which platforms they are using and how they are using them. This can give you insights into what is working for them and help you determine which platforms might be most effective for your business.

Choose the Right Platform

Resources: Consider the resources you have available to manage your social media presence. If you have limited staff time or budget, it might be more practical to focus on just a few platforms rather than trying to manage a presence on every platform.

Platform features: Different social media platforms offer different features and capabilities. For example, Instagram is primarily a visual platform, while Twitter is focused on text-based content. Consider which features and capabilities are most important for your business and choose platforms that align with your needs.

Platform algorithms: Each social media platform has its own algorithm that determines which content is shown to which users. Understanding how these algorithms work can help you optimize your content and reach more of your target audience.

Platform policies: Each social media platform has its own policies and guidelines for content and behavior. Make sure to familiarize yourself with these policies and adhere to them to avoid any potential issues with your account.

Platform demographics: Each social media platform has a unique demographic of users. For example, Facebook tends to have an older user base, while platforms such as TikTok and Instagram are popular with younger audiences. Understanding the demographics of each platform can help you determine which platforms are most likely to reach your target audience.

Choose the Right Platform

Platform trends: Keep an eye on trends and updates on the social media platforms you are using. These can give you insights into new features or changes that could affect your social media marketing efforts.

Platform culture: Each social media platform has its own culture and tone, which can affect the type of content that is most successful on that platform. For example, Instagram tends to be more visual and polished, while Twitter is known for its fast-paced, conversational style.

Platform goals: Consider your overall business and marketing goals when choosing which platforms to focus on. For example, if your goal is to drive traffic to your website, platforms such as Twitter or LinkedIn, which allow for links to be included in posts, might be more effective.

Platform testing: Don't be afraid to experiment with different platforms to see which ones work best for your business. Start by focusing on a few platforms and see how your content performs. You can then adjust your strategy based on your results.

Platform integrations: Many social media platforms offer integrations with other tools and software, such as email marketing platforms or customer relationship management systems. Consider which integrations might be useful for your business and choose platforms that offer the integrations you need.

Choose the Right Platform

Platform advertising options: If you plan to use paid advertising on social media, consider the advertising options available on each platform. Different platforms offer different ad formats, targeting options, and pricing, so it's important to understand the options available and choose platforms that align with your advertising goals and budget.

Platform customer support: Consider the level of customer support available on each platform. If you are new to social media marketing or have limited experience, it might be helpful to choose platforms that offer robust customer support to help you get up and running.

Platform user experience: Consider the user experience on each platform. Is it easy to use? Is the interface intuitive? A good user experience can make it easier to manage your social media marketing efforts and can help you stay engaged with your audience.

Choosing the right social media platforms for your business requires careful consideration and research. By considering factors such as your target audience, business type, resources, competitors, platform features, algorithms, policies, trends, demographics, culture, goals, testing, integrations, advertising options, customer support, and user experience, you can choose platforms that will help you effectively reach and engage with your audience.

Create a Content Plan

A best practice content plan for social media marketing should a mix of content, promotion, monitoring and analysis, staying up to date, incorporation of user-generated content, consideration of seasonality, audience feedback, audience engagement, the use of hashtags, calls to action, storytelling, SEO, social media advertising, influencer partnerships, social media management tools, customer service, social listening, mobile optimization, timing, cross-promotion, collaboration with other businesses, engagement with followers, and measuring and analyzing results. By considering these factors and following best practices, you can create a content plan that helps you achieve your business goals and effectively reach and engage with your target audience.

Plan out the content you will post on each platform. Consider factors such as timing, frequency, and variety when creating your content calendar.

Create a mix of content: Use a variety of content formats, such as text, images, videos, and infographics, to keep your audience engaged.

Promote your content: Use paid advertising and influencer partnerships to help reach a larger audience.

Stay up to date: Keep an eye on industry trends and updates on the social media platforms you are using.

Be consistent and flexible: Maintain a consistent brand voice and style, but also be willing to try new things and experiment with different types of content.

Create a Content Plan

A/B testing: Use A/B testing to help you determine which types of content and formats are most effective for your audience. This involves creating two versions of a piece of content and comparing their performance to see which one performs better.

Repurposing content: Get more value out of your content by repurposing it for different platforms or formats. For example, you can turn a blog post into a series of social media posts, or turn a video into an infographic.

User-generated content: Encourage your audience to create and share content related to your business. User-generated content can help increase engagement and can be a valuable source of content for your social media marketing efforts.

Seasonality: Keep in mind that different types of content may be more relevant at different times of the year. For example, you might create holiday-themed content around the winter holidays or create content related to outdoor activities in the summer.

Audience feedback: Pay attention to feedback from your audience to understand what types of content they find most valuable and engaging. This can help you refine your content plan and create content that resonates with your audience.

Create a Content Plan

Audience engagement: Encourage your audience to interact with your content by asking questions, running polls, or hosting live streams. Engagement can help increase brand awareness and can be a valuable source of feedback and insights.

Hashtags: Use relevant hashtags to help your content reach a larger audience and to make it easier for people to discover your content.

Calls to action: Include calls to action in your content to encourage your audience to take specific actions, such as visiting your website or signing up for your email list.

Visuals: Use visually appealing content, such as images and videos, to help capture your audience's attention.

Storytelling: Consider using storytelling techniques to help make your content more engaging and memorable.

Consistency across platforms: Maintain a consistent brand voice and style across all of your social media platforms.

SEO: Consider optimizing your social media content for search engines to help improve your visibility and reach. This can involve using relevant keywords and including links back to your website.

Social media influencer partnerships: Partner with social media influencers to help promote your content and reach a larger audience.

Create a Content Plan

Social media management tools: Use social media management tools to help you schedule and publish your content, track your results, and monitor your social media activity.

Customer service: Use social media as a customer service channel to help resolve customer issues and answer questions in a timely manner.

Social listening: Use social media monitoring tools to track mentions of your brand and industry keywords and to stay up to date on what people are saying about your business.

Mobile optimization: Make sure that your social media content is optimized for mobile devices to ensure that it looks good and is easy to read on smaller screens.

Timing: Consider the best times to post your content on each social media platform to maximize visibility and engagement.

Cross-promotion: Promote your social media content on other channels, such as your email list or website, to help reach a larger audience.

Engagement with followers: Respond to comments and messages from your followers to build relationships and increase engagement.

Budget

Budget is an important factor to consider when it comes to social media marketing. By setting specific, measurable goals, determining your budget that helps you achieve your business goals and effectively reach and engage with your target audience.

Set specific, measurable goals: Determine what you want to achieve through your social media marketing efforts and allocate your budget accordingly. For example, if your main goal is to increase brand awareness, you may want to allocate a larger budget for paid advertising.

Determine your budget: Consider how much you are willing and able to spend on your social media marketing efforts. Keep in mind that you don't necessarily need a large budget to be successful on social media. There are many tactics, such as organic posting and collaboration, that can be effective without a large budget.

Allocate your budget: Decide how you want to allocate your budget among different tactics and platforms. For example, you may want to allocate a larger budget for paid advertising on one platform and a smaller budget for organic posting on another.

Monitor and adjust your budget: Use data and analytics tools to track the performance of your social media marketing efforts and make adjustments to your budget as needed.

Budget

Cost per action: Consider the cost per action (CPA) of different tactics and platforms. CPA is the cost of a specific action, such as a click, a lead, or a sale. Comparing the CPA of different tactics can help you determine the most cost-effective way to allocate your budget.

Return on investment (ROI): Calculate the return on investment (ROI) of your social media marketing efforts to understand how much value you are getting for your budget. ROI is the amount of profit or benefit you are getting in return for your investment.

Cost-effective tactics: Use cost-effective tactics, such as organic posting and collaboration, to help stretch your budget further.

Budgeting for paid advertising: Consider using paid advertising on social media to help reach a larger audience and to target specific demographics or interests. Keep in mind that paid advertising can be more expensive than other tactics, so be sure to carefully consider your budget when deciding how much to allocate for paid advertising.

Cost per impression (CPI): Consider the cost per impression (CPI) of different tactics and platforms. CPI is the cost of reaching 1,000 people with your content. Comparing the CPI of different tactics can help you determine the most cost-effective way to allocate your budget.

Budget

Testing and optimization: Use testing and optimization techniques, such as A/B testing and audience targeting, to help improve the performance of your social media marketing efforts and get the most value for your budget.

Cost per click (CPC): Consider the cost per click (CPC) of different tactics and platforms. CPC is the cost of getting a single click on your content. Comparing the CPC of different tactics can help you determine the most cost-effective way to allocate your budget.

Cost per lead (CPL): Consider the cost per lead (CPL) of different tactics and platforms. CPL is the cost of generating a single lead, such as a sign-up for your email list or a request for more information. Comparing the CPL of different tactics can help you determine the most cost-effective way to allocate your budget.

Cost per acquisition (CPA): Consider the cost per acquisition (CPA) of different tactics and platforms. CPA is the cost of acquiring a single customer. Comparing the CPA of different tactics can help you determine the most cost-effective way to allocate your budget.

Cost per thousand (CPM): Consider the cost per thousand (CPM) of different tactics and platforms. CPM is the cost of reaching 1,000 people with your content. Comparing the CPM of different tactics can help you determine the most cost-effective way to allocate your budget.

Budget

Cost per action (CPA) vs. cost per impression (CPI): While CPA and CPI are both measures of the cost of reaching your audience, CPA is specific to a specific action, such as a click or a sale, while CPI is a measure of the overall reach of your content. As a result, CPI can be a useful measure when your main goal is brand awareness, while CPA is more useful when your main goal is conversions.

Cost per lead (CPL) vs. cost per acquisition (CPA): CPL is a measure of the cost of generating a single lead, while CPA is a measure of the cost of acquiring a single customer. CPL can be a useful measure when your main goal is to generate leads, while CPA is more useful when your main goal is to acquire customers.

Testing and optimization: Use testing and optimization techniques, such as A/B testing and audience targeting, to help improve the performance of your social media marketing efforts and get the most value for your budget. By testing different tactics and targeting different audiences, you can identify which strategies are most effective and allocate your budget accordingly.

Flexibility: Be flexible with your budget and be prepared to make adjustments as needed based on your results. For example, if a particular tactic or platform is not performing well, consider reallocating your budget to other tactics or platforms that are more effective.

Resources

The Power of Resources in Social Media Marketing

Social media has become an essential marketing tool for businesses of all sizes. According to Statista, there were 4.96 billion social media users worldwide in 2022, and this number is expected to continue growing in the coming years. With such a large and diverse audience, social media offers a powerful opportunity for businesses to reach and engage with their target customers.

However, to effectively leverage the power of social media, businesses need to allocate their resources wisely. In this article, we'll explore the various resources that businesses can use to support their social media marketing efforts, and we'll provide tips for using these resources effectively to achieve your business goals.

What Are the Resources for Social Media Marketing?

There are a variety of resources that businesses can use to support their social media marketing efforts. Here are a few examples:

Social media management tools: Use social media management tools to help you schedule and publish your content, track your results, and monitor your social media activity. Some popular social media management tools include Hootsuite, Buffer, and Sprout Social.

Resources

Social media monitoring tools: Use social media monitoring tools to track mentions of your brand and industry keywords and to stay up to date on what people are saying about your business. Some popular social media monitoring tools include Hootsuite, Mention, and Brand24.

Analytics and data tools: Use analytics and data tools, such as Google Analytics and Facebook Insights, to track the performance of your social media marketing efforts and to make data-driven decisions.

Social media advertising: Use paid social media advertising to help reach a larger audience and to target specific demographics or interests. Some popular social media advertising platforms include Facebook Ads, Instagram Ads, and Twitter Ads.

Influencer partnerships: Partner with influencers to help promote your brand and reach a larger audience. Influencers are individuals who have a large following on social media and can help you reach a specific target audience.

Social listening: Use social listening tools to track mentions of your brand and industry keywords and to stay up to date on what people are saying about your business. Social listening can help you identify opportunities for engagement, as well as potential issues or concerns that you can address.

Resources

Content creation tools: Use content creation tools, such as Canva, Piktochart, and Adobe Creative Suite, to help you create visually appealing content for your social media channels.

Collaboration: Collaborate with other businesses or organizations to co-create and co-promote content. Collaboration can help you reach a larger audience and can be a cost-effective way to support your social media marketing efforts.

User-generated content: Encourage your followers to share their own content related to your brand or industry. User-generated content can help you create a sense of community and can be a powerful way to showcase the value of your products or services.

Social media policies: Develop a social media policy to guide your social media activity and set clear expectations for how your business will use social media. A social media policy can help you protect your brand reputation and ensure that your social media activity aligns with your business goals.

Social media training: Provide social media training to your employees to ensure that they are aware of your social media policies and are able to effectively represent your brand on social media.

Social media integration: Integrate your social media activity with other marketing channels and touchpoints, such as your website, email marketing, and customer service, to create a seamless customer experience.

Resources

Social media editorial calendar: Use a social media editorial calendar to plan and schedule your content in advance based on a specific theme or focus. An editorial calendar can help you ensure that your content is relevant and consistent with your business goals.

Social media guidelines: Develop social media guidelines to set clear expectations for how your business will use social media. Social media guidelines can include guidelines for tone, language, content, and behavior on social media.

Social media roles and responsibilities: Define roles and responsibilities for social media activity within your organization. This can include roles for social media strategy, content creation, community management, and measurement and analysis.

Social media metrics: Use social media metrics to track the performance of your social media marketing efforts and to understand the impact of your social media activity on your business goals. Some common social media metrics include reach, engagement, followers, leads, and conversions.

Social media KPIs: Identify key performance indicators (KPIs) to help measure the success of your social media marketing efforts and to understand the impact of your social media activity on your business goals. Your social media KPIs should be aligned with your social media objectives and should be specific, measurable, and actionable.

Resources

Social media reporting: Use social media reporting tools and techniques to track the performance of your social media marketing efforts and to understand the impact of your social media activity on your business goals. Social media reporting can help you identify trends, patterns, and opportunities for improvement.

Social media analytics: Use social media analytics tools and techniques to track the performance of your social media marketing efforts and to understand the impact of your social media activity on your business goals. Social media analytics can help you identify trends, patterns, and opportunities for improvement.

Social media ROI: Calculate the return on investment (ROI) of your social media marketing efforts to understand the impact of your social media activity on your business goals. To calculate social media ROI, you can divide the value of your social media activity (such as sales or leads generated) by the cost of your social media efforts (such as advertising or labor).

Social media governance: Implement a social media governance framework to help ensure that your social media activity is consistent, compliant, and aligned with your business goals. A social media governance framework can include guidelines, policies, procedures, and roles and responsibilities for social media activity.

Resources

Use Cost-Effective Tactics

To stretch your resources further, consider using cost-effective tactics, such as organic content, influencer partnerships, and user-generated content. These tactics can help you reach and engage with your target audience without requiring a large budget.

Use a Mix of Paid and Organic Tactics

Paid tactics, such as social media advertising, can help you reach a larger audience and target specific demographics or interests. However, it's important to also use organic tactics, such as content marketing and social media engagement, to build trust and credibility with your audience. A mix of paid and organic tactics can help you achieve a balance between reach and engagement.

By following these tips, you can effectively allocate your resources and use them to reach and engage with your target audience and achieve your business goals through social media marketing.

Integration with Other Marketing Efforts

The Power of Integration in Social Media Marketing

Social media offers a powerful opportunity for businesses to reach and engage with their target customers. However, to effectively leverage the power of social media, businesses need to integrate their social media activity with other marketing efforts.

In this article, we'll explore the benefits of integration in social media marketing, and we'll provide tips for integrating your social media activity with other marketing channels and touchpoints to achieve your business goals.

The Benefits of Integration in Social Media Marketing

Integration in social media marketing refers to the practice of aligning and integrating your social media activity with other marketing channels and touchpoints, such as your website, email marketing, and customer service.

There are several benefits to integration in social media marketing:

Improved customer experience: Integration helps create a seamless customer experience across all marketing channels and touchpoints. By aligning your social media activity with other marketing efforts, you can provide a consistent and cohesive message to your customers and create a more cohesive brand experience.

Integration with Other Marketing Efforts

Increased brand awareness: Integration can help increase brand awareness by showcasing your brand consistently across various marketing channels and touchpoints. By aligning your social media activity with other marketing efforts, you can create a more cohesive and recognizable brand image.

Improved customer engagement: Integration can help improve customer engagement by providing customers with multiple touchpoints to interact with your brand. By aligning your social media activity with other marketing efforts, you can create a more engaging and interactive brand experience.

Increased website traffic: Integration can help increase website traffic by driving traffic from your social media channels to your website. By aligning your social media activity with other marketing efforts, you can create a more integrated and cohesive marketing strategy that helps drive traffic to your website.

Integration with Other Marketing Efforts

Tips for Integrating Your Social Media Marketing Efforts

Align your messaging: Ensure that your messaging is consistent and aligned across all marketing channels and touchpoints. This includes your brand voice, tone, and messaging.

Use social media to drive traffic to your website: Use your social media channels to drive traffic to your website by linking to your website in your social media posts and by promoting your website through social media advertising.

Integrate social media with email marketing: Integrate your social media activity with your email marketing efforts by including social media icons in your email signature, promoting your email newsletter on social media, and using email marketing to drive traffic to your social media channels.

Use social media for customer service: Use your social media channels as a platform for customer service by responding to customer inquiries, complaints, and feedback in a timely and professional manner.

Integrate social media with your website: Integrate your social media activity with your website by including social media icons and links on your website, embedding social media feeds on your website, and promoting your website through social media advertising.

Integration with Other Marketing Efforts

Use social media to support offline marketing efforts:
Integrate your social media activity with offline marketing efforts, such as events, trade shows, and in-store promotions, by promoting these activities on social media and using social media to drive traffic to offline events.

Use social media to support paid advertising efforts:
Integrate your social media activity with paid advertising efforts by aligning your social media messaging with your paid advertising campaigns and using social media to promote and drive traffic to your paid advertising.

Use cross-channel promotion: Promote your social media channels on other marketing channels and vice versa. For example, include social media icons and links on your email marketing campaigns and promote your email newsletter on social media.

Use social media to support content marketing efforts:
Integrate your social media activity with your content marketing efforts by promoting your blog posts, articles, and other content on social media and using social media to drive traffic to your content.

Use social media to support lead generation efforts:
Integrate your social media activity with your lead generation efforts by using social media to promote lead magnets, such as ebooks, webinars, and whitepapers, and using social media to drive traffic to your lead generation forms.

Integration with Other Marketing Efforts

Use social media to support customer retention efforts: Integrate your social media activity with your customer retention efforts by using social media to engage with and retain your existing customers.

Use social media to support customer loyalty efforts: Integrate your social media activity with your customer loyalty efforts by using social media to reward and recognize your loyal customers.

Use social media to support public relations efforts: Integrate your social media activity with your public relations efforts by using social media to promote press releases, news, and media coverage.

Use social media to support affiliate marketing efforts: Integrate your social media activity with your affiliate marketing efforts by using social media to promote affiliate products and using social media to drive traffic to your affiliate links.

Use social media to support influencer marketing efforts: Integrate your social media activity with your influencer marketing efforts by using social media to promote influencer content and using social media to drive traffic to influencer profiles and pages.

Use social media to support paid search efforts: Integrate your social media activity with your paid search efforts by aligning your social media messaging with your paid search campaigns and using social media to promote and drive traffic to your paid search ads.

Branding

The Importance of Branding in Social Media Marketing

Branding is an essential aspect of any marketing strategy, and social media is no exception. To effectively leverage the power of social media, businesses need to have a strong and consistent brand identity.

In this article, we'll explore the importance of branding in social media marketing, and we'll provide tips for building a strong, cohesive and consistent brand identity on social media.

Why is Branding Important in Social Media Marketing?

Branding is important in social media marketing because it helps businesses create a cohesive and recognizable image that reflects their values, mission, and vision. A strong brand identity helps businesses differentiate themselves from competitors, build trust and credibility with their target audience, and create a lasting impression with customers.

Branding refers to the practice of creating a cohesive and consistent image of your business across all marketing channels and touchpoints. This includes everything from your logo, brand colors, and font choices to your brand messaging, tone, and values.

Branding

Here are a few benefits of branding in social media marketing:

Increased brand awareness: Social media is a powerful tool for building brand awareness. By consistently posting high-quality content and engaging with your target audience on social media, you can increase brand awareness and reach a wider audience.

Improved customer loyalty: A strong and consistent brand identity helps build customer loyalty by creating a sense of trust and familiarity with customers. Customers are more likely to continue doing business with brands they trust and recognize.

Increased customer engagement: A strong and consistent brand identity helps increase customer engagement by creating a cohesive and recognizable image that resonates with customers. Customers are more likely to engage with brands that align with their values and interests.

Improved customer experience: A strong and consistent brand identity helps improve the customer experience by creating a cohesive and cohesive brand experience across all marketing channels and touchpoints. Customers are more likely to have a positive experience with brands that provide a consistent and cohesive message.

Branding

Tips for Building a Strong and Consistent Brand Identity on Social Media

Define your brand: Clearly define your brand by creating a brand strategy that outlines your brand's mission, vision, values, and target audience.

Create a visual identity: Develop a visual identity that reflects your brand's personality and values. This includes your logo, color scheme, font, and imagery.

Post high-quality content: Consistently post high-quality content that aligns with your brand's mission, vision, and values. This includes text, images, videos, and other forms of content.

Monitor and track your brand performance: Monitor and track your brand performance by using social media analytics tools to measure the reach and engagement of your content, as well as the sentiment of your audience.

Develop a clear brand voice: Develop a clear brand voice that reflects your business values and personality. Use this brand voice consistently across all your social media posts to create a consistent and cohesive brand image.

Create a clear brand messaging: Develop a clear brand messaging that reflects your business values and mission. Use this brand messaging consistently across all your social media posts to create a consistent and cohesive brand image.

Branding

Engage with your audience: Engage with your audience on social media by responding to comments, feedback, and inquiries in a timely and professional manner. This helps build trust and loyalty with your customers and creates a more cohesive and interactive brand experience.

Use hashtags consistently: Use relevant and consistent hashtags in your social media posts to help increase brand visibility and create a cohesive brand image.

Use storytelling: Use storytelling techniques, such as customer stories, case studies, and behind-the-scenes content, to help create a more engaging and cohesive brand image on social media.

Tell your brand story: Use social media to tell your brand story and share the values, mission, and personality of your business. This helps create a more personal and cohesive brand image.

Use user-generated content: Encourage your customers to share their own experiences and content related to your brand on social media. This can help create a more authentic and cohesive brand image.

Use social media contests and promotions: Use social media contests and promotions to help increase engagement and reach on social media.

Use social media to build relationships: Use social media to build relationships with your customers by engaging with them and creating a personalized and interactive brand experience.

Branding

Use social media to create a sense of community: Use social media to create a sense of community and encourage your customers to share their experiences and feedback with your business. This helps create a more cohesive and interactive brand image.

By following these tips, you can effectively create a strong and cohesive brand on social media, which can improve customer recognition, increase brand awareness, improve customer trust, and improve customer loyalty.

Tone of Voice

The Importance of a Brand's Tone in Marketing

In today's competitive and crowded online landscape, it's more important than ever for businesses to differentiate themselves and stand out from their competitors. One way to do this is by developing a strong and cohesive brand tone.

A brand's tone refers to the overall personality and character of the brand as communicated through its messaging and content. A strong brand tone helps establish credibility, trust, and loyalty with your customers, which can improve customer recognition, increase brand awareness, and increase customer loyalty.

In this article, we'll explore the importance of a brand's tone in marketing and we'll provide tips for developing a strong brand tone.

Tips for Developing a Strong Brand Tone

Use tone appropriately: Use tone appropriately based on the context of your messaging and the audience you are targeting. For example, if you are targeting a younger audience, you may want to use a more casual and playful tone, while if you are targeting a more formal audience, you may want to use a more professional and formal tone.

Test your tone: Test different tones to see which one resonates best with your target audience. You can do this through A/B testing or by gathering feedback from your customers.

Tone of Voice

Convey your brand values: Use your brand tone to convey your brand values and mission to your customers. This helps establish credibility and trust with your customers.

Reflect your brand personality: Use your brand tone to reflect the overall personality of your brand and create a cohesive and consistent brand image. For example, if your brand values sustainability and environmental responsibility, you may want to use a more environmentally-conscious tone in your messaging.

Differentiate your brand: Use your brand tone to differentiate your brand from your competitors and create a unique and memorable brand image. For example, if your competitors are using a more formal and serious tone, you may want to differentiate your brand by using a more casual and playful tone.

Create a sense of emotion: Use tone to create a sense of emotion and connect with your customers on a deeper level. For example, if your brand values empathy and compassion, you may want to use a more caring and sympathetic tone in your messaging.

Create a sense of trust: Use tone to create a sense of trust and demonstrate to your customers that you are a reliable and trustworthy business. For example, if your brand values honesty and transparency, you may want to use a straightforward and transparent tone in your messaging.

Tone of Voice

Connect with your audience: Use your brand tone to connect with your audience and create a personalized and interactive brand experience.

Create a sense of excitement: Use tone to create a sense of excitement and energize your customers. For example, if your brand values innovation and creativity, you may want to use an energetic and innovative tone in your messaging.

Create a sense of community: Use tone to create a sense of community and encourage your customers to engage with your brand. For example, if your brand values inclusivity and collaboration, you may want to use a welcoming and collaborative tone in your messaging.

By following these tips, you can effectively develop a strong and cohesive brand tone that reflects your brand values, mission, and target audience. This can help improve customer recognition, increase brand awareness, improve customer trust, and improve customer loyalty.

Engagement

Social media allows businesses to connect with their customers in real-time and create a personalized and interactive brand experience.

In this article, we'll explore the importance of engagement in social media marketing and we'll provide tips for increasing engagement on social media.

Engagement refers to the level of interaction and participation between a business and its customers on social media. Engagement is important in social media marketing because it helps create a personalized and interactive brand experience, which can improve customer loyalty and retention.

Tips for Increasing Engagement on Social Media

Here are a few tips for increasing engagement on social media:

Be responsive: Be responsive to your customers' comments and feedback on social media. This demonstrates to your customers that you value their opinions and concerns, which can improve customer trust and loyalty.

Use interactive content: Use interactive content, such as polls, quizzes, or questions, to encourage your customers to engage with your brand on social media.

Use visuals: Use visuals, such as images, videos, or GIFs, to grab the attention of your customers and encourage them to engage with your brand on social media.

Collaboration

Collaboration is important in social media marketing because it helps increase brand visibility, credibility, and reach.

Benefits of collaboration in social media marketing

Increased brand visibility: Collaboration helps increase brand visibility by reaching a larger audience and leveraging the reach and influence of other businesses and influencers. By collaborating with other businesses and influencers on social media, you can increase the visibility and reach of your brand, which can lead to increased brand awareness and customer acquisition.

Improved brand credibility: Collaboration helps improve brand credibility by leveraging the influence and credibility of other businesses and influencers. By collaborating with other businesses and influencers on social media, you can demonstrate to your customers that your brand is trusted and respected by others in your industry, which can improve customer trust and loyalty.

Increased brand reach: Collaboration helps increase brand reach by leveraging the audience and influence of other businesses and influencers. By collaborating with other businesses and influencers on social media, you can reach a larger and more targeted audience, which can lead to increased brand reach and customer acquisition.

Overall, collaboration is an effective way to increase brand visibility, credibility, and reach on social media, which can lead to improved customer loyalty, increased brand awareness, and improved customer retention.

Collaboration

Tips for Effectively Collaborating on Social Media

Identify potential collaborators: Identify potential collaborators, such as other businesses or influencers in your industry, that align with your brand values and mission. Research their social media presence and audience to determine if they would be a good fit for your brand.

Reach out to potential collaborators: Reach out to potential collaborators and pitch your collaboration idea. Be sure to clearly outline the benefits of the collaboration and how it will benefit both parties. Consider offering incentives, such as a discount or promotion, to encourage their participation.

Negotiate terms: Negotiate the terms of the collaboration, such as the duration, frequency, and type of content to be shared. Be sure to clearly communicate your expectations and goals for the collaboration.

Create a collaboration plan: Create a collaboration plan that outlines the details of the collaboration, such as the content to be shared, the frequency of the collaboration, and any promotional efforts. Consider using tools, such as a project management software or shared Google Doc, to help manage the collaboration.

Evaluate the success of the collaboration: Evaluate the success of the collaboration by tracking the performance of the collaboration and gathering feedback from your customers. Use this information to identify any areas for improvement and to optimize future collaborations.

Collaboration

Use social media analytics: Use social media analytics tools, such as Facebook Insights or Twitter Analytics, to track the performance of your collaboration and identify the types of content that are most engaging to your audience.

Create unique and engaging content: Create unique and engaging content for your collaboration to help increase brand visibility and credibility. This could include blog posts, infographics, videos, or other types of content that are relevant to your brand and industry.

Promote your collaboration: Promote your collaboration on social media and other marketing channels to help increase brand visibility and reach. This could include sharing updates on your collaboration, running social media ads, or promoting your collaboration on your website or email newsletters.

Engage with your audience: Engage with your audience during and after the collaboration to encourage customer engagement and participation. This could include answering questions, responding to comments, or sharing user-generated content.

Foster long-term relationships: Foster long-term relationships with your collaborators by continuing to engage with them on social media and exploring potential future collaborations. This can help increase brand visibility and credibility over time.

Social Media Marketing Tools

Social media tools are software or platforms that help businesses manage and optimize their social media marketing efforts. These tools can help businesses automate and streamline their social media tasks, track their social media performance, and create and schedule content.

A few types of social media tools that businesses can use:

Social media management tools: Social media management tools help businesses manage and optimize their social media presence across multiple platforms. These tools can help businesses schedule and publish content, respond to customer inquiries, and track the performance of their social media campaigns. Examples of social media management tools include Hootsuite, Buffer, and Sprout Social.

Social media analytics tools: Social media analytics tools help businesses track the performance of their social media campaigns and identify areas for improvement. These tools can provide insights into a variety of metrics, such as reach, engagement, and audience demographics. Examples of social media analytics tools include Facebook Insights, Twitter Analytics, and Instagram Insights.

Social media scheduling tools: Social media scheduling tools help businesses schedule and publish content on social media in advance. These tools can help businesses save time and ensure a consistent posting schedule. Examples of social media scheduling tools include Hootsuite, Buffer, and Later.

Social Media Marketing Tools

Social media listening tools: Social media listening tools help businesses monitor social media platforms for mentions of their brand, competitors, or relevant keywords. These tools can help businesses track customer sentiment and identify opportunities for engagement. Examples of social media listening tools include Hootsuite, Mention, and Brand24.

Social media advertising tools: Social media advertising tools help businesses create and manage social media ad campaigns. These tools can help businesses target specific audiences and track the performance of their ads. Examples of social media advertising tools include Facebook Ads Manager, Twitter Ads, and LinkedIn Ads.

By using social media tools, businesses can save time, improve their social media performance, and create a more efficient and effective social media marketing strategy. It's important for businesses to research and choose the right tools for their needs, as different tools may offer different features and capabilities. By using the right social media tools, businesses can better manage and optimize their social media marketing efforts and achieve their marketing goals.

Social Media Marketing Tools

Streamline social media tasks, track social media performance, and create and schedule content. These tools can save businesses time and improve their social media performance, which can lead to increased brand visibility, credibility, and reach.

Benefits of using social media tools include:

Time-saving: Social media tools can help businesses automate and streamline their social media tasks, such as scheduling and publishing content, responding to customer inquiries, and tracking the performance of their social media campaigns. This can save businesses time and allow them to focus on other aspects of their business.

Improved social media performance: Social media tools, such as social media analytics and social media listening tools, can help businesses track the performance of their social media campaigns and identify areas for improvement. By using these tools, businesses can optimize their social media strategy and increase their reach and engagement on social media.

Consistent posting schedule: Social media scheduling tools can help businesses schedule and publish content on social media in advance. This can help businesses maintain a consistent posting schedule, which can improve brand visibility and credibility.

Social Media Marketing Tools

Increased reach and targeting: Social media advertising tools can help businesses create and manage social media ad campaigns, which can help increase brand reach and target specific audiences.

Customization and integration: Many social media tools offer customization and integration options, which can help businesses tailor their social media strategy to their specific needs and goals. For example, businesses can use tools that integrate with their CRM or email marketing software to create a more cohesive and efficient marketing strategy.

Competitive advantage: By using social media tools, businesses can gain a competitive advantage over their competitors by staying up-to-date on industry trends, analyzing their social media performance, and optimizing their social media strategy.

Cost-effectiveness: Many social media tools offer a range of pricing options, including free and paid plans, which can help businesses find the right tools for their budget. By using social media tools, businesses can save time and resources, which can lead to cost-savings in the long run.

Improved customer experience: By using social media tools, businesses can improve the customer experience on social media by responding to customer inquiries quickly and consistently, tracking customer sentiment, and creating personalized and engaging content. This can improve customer loyalty and trust, which can lead to increased brand loyalty and customer retention.

Social Media Marketing Tools

Tips for effectively using social media tools:

Research and choose the right tools: There are many different social media tools available, so it's important to research and choose the right tools for your business's specific needs and goals. Consider factors such as your budget, the type of social media platforms you use, and the features and capabilities that are important to your business.

Set up and customize your tools: Once you've chosen your social media tools, set them up and customize them to suit your business's needs. This may include connecting your social media accounts, integrating with other marketing software, and customizing your settings and preferences.

Create and schedule content: Use social media scheduling tools to create and schedule content for your social media platforms. This can help you save time and ensure a consistent posting schedule.

Track and analyze your performance: Use social media analytics tools to track the performance of your social media campaigns and identify areas for improvement. This can help you optimize your social media strategy and increase your reach and engagement on social media.

Monitor and respond to customer inquiries: Use social media management tools to monitor your social media accounts for customer inquiries and respond to them promptly and consistently. This can help improve the customer experience and build customer loyalty and trust.

Social Media Marketing Tools

Use social media listening tools to track mentions of your brand, competitors, or relevant keywords on social media. This can help you track customer sentiment and identify opportunities for engagement.

Use social media advertising tools to create and manage social media ad campaigns. These tools can help you target specific audiences and track the performance of your ads.

Integrate your social media tools with your other marketing efforts to create a cohesive and efficient marketing strategy. For example, you can integrate your social media tools with your email marketing software or CRM to create a more seamless customer experience.

Stay up-to-date on the latest features and capabilities of your social media tools. Many social media tools regularly update their features and capabilities, so it's important to keep track of these updates and see how they can benefit your business.

Consider using a social media marketing agency or professional to help you effectively use and optimize your social media tools. These professionals can provide expertise and guidance on how to best use social media tools to achieve your marketing goals.

By following these tips, you can effectively use social media tools to manage and optimize your social media marketing efforts and achieve your marketing goals.

Social Media Marketing Tools

There are many other tools available, so it's important for businesses to research and choose the right tools for their specific needs and goals.

Hootsuite: A social media management tool that helps businesses manage and optimize their social media presence across multiple platforms.

Buffer: A social media management and scheduling tool that helps businesses schedule and publish content on social media.

Sprout Social: A social media management tool that helps businesses manage and optimize their social media presence across multiple platforms.

Facebook Insights: A social media analytics tool that provides insights into a business's Facebook performance.

Twitter Analytics: A social media analytics tool that provides insights into a business's Twitter performance.

Instagram Insights: A social media analytics tool that provides insights into a business's Instagram performance.

Later: A social media scheduling tool that helps businesses schedule and publish content on social media.

Mention: A social media listening tool that helps businesses monitor social media platforms for mentions of their brand, competitors, or relevant keywords.

Social Media Marketing Tools

Brand24: A social media listening tool that helps businesses monitor social media platforms for mentions of their brand, competitors, or relevant keywords.

Facebook Ads Manager: A social media advertising tool that helps businesses create and manage Facebook ad campaigns.

Twitter Ads: A social media advertising tool that helps businesses create and manage Twitter ad campaigns.

LinkedIn Ads: A social media advertising tool that helps businesses create and manage LinkedIn ad campaigns.

Google Ads: A social media advertising tool that helps businesses create and manage Google ad campaigns.

Pinterest Ads: A social media advertising tool that helps businesses create and manage Pinterest ad campaigns.

AdEspresso: A social media advertising tool that helps businesses create and optimize ad campaigns on multiple platforms.

Canva: A design tool that helps businesses create visually appealing social media graphics and other marketing materials.

Adobe Creative Cloud: A suite of design and creative tools that helps businesses create marketing materials for social media and other platforms.

Social Media Marketing Tools

Piktochart: A design tool that helps businesses create infographics and other visual content for social media.

CoSchedule Headline Analyzer: A tool that helps businesses create compelling and SEO-friendly headlines for their social media content.

Grammarly: A writing tool that helps businesses improve the grammar and spelling of their social media content.

MeetEdgar: A social media management and scheduling tool that helps businesses schedule and publish content on social media and recycle old content.

Klout: A social media analytics tool that measures a business's influence on social media.

Socialbakers: A social media analytics and management tool that helps businesses track the performance of their social media campaigns and optimize their strategy.

TweetDeck: A social media management tool that helps businesses manage and optimize their Twitter presence.

SocialOomph: A social media management and scheduling tool that helps businesses schedule and publish content on social media and automate certain tasks.

Agorapulse: A social media management and analytics tool that helps businesses manage and optimize their social media presence across multiple platforms.

Social Media Marketing Tools

Zoho Social: A social media management and analytics tool that helps businesses manage and optimize their social media presence across multiple platforms.

Sendible: A social media management and analytics tool that helps businesses manage and optimize their social media presence across multiple platforms.

Digimind: A social media listening and analytics tool that helps businesses track and analyze mentions of their brand, competitors, or relevant keywords on social media.

NetBase: A social media listening and analytics tool that helps businesses track and analyze mentions of their brand, competitors, or relevant keywords on social media.

BrandMentions: A social media listening tool that helps businesses track and analyze mentions of their brand, competitors, or relevant keywords on social media.

Sprinklr: A social media management and analytics tool that helps businesses manage and optimize their social media presence across multiple platforms.

SocialFlow: A social media management and analytics tool that helps businesses optimize their content distribution on social media.

Google Analytics: A web analytics tool that helps businesses track and analyze the performance of their social media and other online marketing efforts.

Social Media Marketing Tools

Crazy Egg: A website analytics tool that helps businesses track and analyze the performance of their social media and other online marketing efforts.

Hotjar: A website analytics and user feedback tool that helps businesses track and analyze the performance of their social media and other online marketing efforts.

SumoMe: A suite of marketing tools that helps businesses optimize their social media and other online marketing efforts.

OptinMonster: A lead generation and conversion optimization tool that helps businesses improve the performance of their social media and other online marketing efforts.

Leadpages: A lead generation and conversion optimization tool that helps businesses improve the performance of their social media and other online marketing efforts.

Unbounce: A lead generation and conversion optimization tool that helps businesses improve the performance of their social media and other online marketing efforts.

Employee Advocacy

Employee advocacy is the practice of encouraging and enabling employees to promote and support their employer's brand, products, and services on social media and other online platforms. This can involve employees sharing company content, sharing their own content related to their employer's brand, or engaging with customers and followers on social media.

There are several benefits to implementing employee advocacy in a business's social media marketing strategy.

First, employee advocacy can help increase a brand's reach and visibility on social media. When employees share content and engage with their followers, it can expose the brand to a new and potentially larger audience.

Second, employee advocacy can help build trust and credibility for a brand. When employees share content and engage with their followers, it can be seen as more authentic and genuine than content shared solely by the brand. This can help build trust and credibility with potential customers and clients.

Third, employee advocacy can help improve employee engagement and morale. When employees are empowered and encouraged to share their thoughts and experiences on social media, it can help improve their engagement and satisfaction with their job. This can lead to increased productivity and loyalty to the company.

Employee Advocacy

Clearly define the goals and expectations for employee advocacy. This can include things like the types of content that employees should share, the tone and voice they should use, and the frequency of their engagement.

Provide training and resources to employees: This can include training on the company's social media policies and guidelines, as well as resources such as branded graphics and pre-approved content for employees to share.

Encourage and reward employee participation: This can include recognizing and rewarding employees who actively participate in employee advocacy, or creating incentives for employees to engage on social media.

Establish clear guidelines and policies: It's important for businesses to establish clear guidelines and policies for employee advocacy to ensure that employees understand what is expected of them and to protect the company's reputation. These guidelines should outline the types of content that employees can share, the tone and voice they should use, and any other rules or expectations for employee engagement on social media.

Encourage authenticity: While it's important for employees to support and promote the company's brand, it's also important for them to be authentic in their engagement on social media. Encourage employees to share their own thoughts and experiences related to the company's products and services, rather than simply promoting the company's messaging.

Employee Advocacy

Monitor and measure the results: Use social media analytics tools to track the performance of employee advocacy efforts and identify areas for improvement. This can help businesses identify which employees are most effective at promoting the company's brand and which types of content are most effective in driving engagement.

Foster a culture of transparency: Encourage employees to be transparent in their engagement on social media. This can include disclosing any conflicts of interest, such as receiving free products or services in exchange for a review.

By following these best practices, businesses can ensure that their employee advocacy efforts are successful and contribute to the overall success of their social media marketing strategy.

Social Media Policies

Social media policies are guidelines and rules that businesses establish for employee use of social media. These policies can cover a wide range of topics, including the types of content that employees can share, the tone and voice they should use, and the frequency of their engagement on social media. Social media policies are designed to protect the company's reputation, ensure compliance with legal and regulatory requirements, and provide guidance to employees on how to effectively use social media to promote and support the company's brand.

Key Components

Purpose and scope: Clearly define the purpose and scope of the social media policy, including which employees are covered by the policy and the types of social media platforms and activities that are covered.

Responsibilities and expectations: Outline the responsibilities and expectations for employee use of social media, including the types of content that can be shared, the tone and voice that should be used, and the frequency of engagement.

Confidentiality: Establish guidelines for the protection of confidential and proprietary information, including company and customer data.

Brand representation: Outline guidelines for the representation of the company's brand on social media, including the use of company logos and branding materials.

Social Media Policies

Disciplinary actions: Clearly outline the consequences for employees who violate the social media policy, including any disciplinary actions that may be taken.

Balancing employee freedom and company control: It's important for businesses to establish clear guidelines and expectations for employee use of social media, while also allowing employees some freedom to express their own thoughts and opinions. Striking the right balance between company control and employee freedom can be challenging.

Ensuring compliance with legal and regulatory requirements: There are a number of legal and regulatory requirements that businesses must comply with when it comes to employee use of social media, including laws related to privacy, data protection, and employment. Ensuring compliance with these requirements can be complex and time-consuming.

Managing employee engagement: Some employees may be enthusiastic about using social media to promote and support the company's brand, while others may be less inclined to engage on social media. It can be challenging for businesses to encourage and motivate all employees to participate in social media marketing efforts.

Measuring the effectiveness of social media policies: It can be difficult for businesses to accurately measure the impact of their social media policies on the company's overall social media marketing strategy.

Social Media Policies

Best practices for businesses to consider when developing and implementing their social media policies:

Involve all relevant stakeholders: When developing a social media policy, it's important to involve all relevant stakeholders, including legal, HR, and marketing departments. This can help ensure that the policy is comprehensive and covers all necessary areas.

Communicate the policy clearly: Clearly communicate the social media policy to all employees, including any updates or changes to the policy. It's important that all employees are aware of and understand the policy and their responsibilities under it.

Train employees on the policy: Provide training to employees on the social media policy and the proper use of social media to promote and support the company's brand. This can help ensure that all employees are aware of and understand the policy and are able to effectively use social media on behalf of the company.

Monitor and enforce the policy: Regularly monitor employee activity on social media to ensure compliance with the policy. Take appropriate disciplinary action as needed for any employees who violate the policy

. ***Review and update the policy regularly:*** It's important to regularly review and update the social media policy to ensure that it remains relevant and effective. This may include updating the policy to reflect changes in the company's business or industry, as well as changes in relevant legal and regulatory requirements.

Crisis Management

Crisis management is the process of identifying, responding to, and mitigating the impact of a crisis on an organization. In the context of social media marketing, crisis management involves developing strategies and tactics to effectively respond to negative events or situations that have the potential to damage the company's reputation or brand image.

There are several key steps that businesses can follow to effectively manage a crisis on social media:

Develop a crisis management plan: Develop a comprehensive crisis management plan that outlines the steps that should be taken in the event of a crisis. This plan should include a list of key stakeholders, a plan for communication and messaging, and a process for monitoring and responding to social media activity.

Monitor social media activity: Regularly monitor social media activity to identify any potential crises or negative events that may impact the company's reputation. Use social media analytics tools to track mentions of the company and its products or services, and monitor social media conversations and trends related to the company.

Respond quickly and transparently: In the event of a crisis, it's important to respond quickly and transparently to address any concerns or issues that may have arisen. Use social media to communicate with customers and stakeholders, provide updates, and address any questions or concerns.

Crisis Management

Stay consistent with messaging: Ensure that all communications and messaging related to the crisis are consistent and aligned with the company's brand and values. This can help to build trust and credibility with customers and stakeholders.

Evaluate and learn from the crisis: After a crisis has been successfully managed, it's important to evaluate the response and identify any areas for improvement. Use this information to update and refine the crisis management plan for future situations.

Involve all relevant stakeholders: When developing a crisis management plan, it's important to involve all relevant stakeholders, including legal, HR, and marketing departments. This can help ensure that the plan is comprehensive and covers all necessary areas.

Establish a clear chain of command: Clearly define the roles and responsibilities of all stakeholders in the crisis management plan, including who is responsible for monitoring and responding to social media activity and who has the authority to make decisions related to the crisis.

Practice and test the crisis management plan: Regularly practice and test the crisis management plan to ensure that all stakeholders are familiar with their roles and responsibilities and that the plan is effective.

Crisis Management

Use a consistent and professional tone: Use a consistent and professional tone in all communications and messaging related to the crisis. Avoid using language or messaging that could be perceived as defensive or aggressive.

Apologize and take responsibility: If appropriate, apologize for any mistakes or errors that may have contributed to the crisis. Take responsibility for the situation and provide a clear plan for addressing and resolving it.

Seek help if needed: If the crisis is beyond the scope of the company's resources or expertise, consider seeking help from outside experts or organizations.

By following these strategies, businesses can effectively manage a crisis on social media and minimize the impact on their reputation and brand image.

Timing

Timing is an important factor in social media marketing because it can have a significant impact on the reach and effectiveness of a campaign. When a social media post or campaign is timed correctly, it is more likely to be seen by a larger audience and to generate more engagement.

For example, if a social media post is made at a time when a business's target audience is most active on social media, it is more likely to be seen and shared. Similarly, if a social media campaign is launched at a time when there is less competition for attention, it is more likely to stand out and be noticed by users.

Timing is also important because it can impact the performance of a social media campaign in relation to algorithms on different platforms. Each social media platform has its own algorithms that determine when and how often a post will be shown to users. By understanding these algorithms and posting at times when posts are more likely to be shown to users, businesses can increase the reach and effectiveness of their marketing efforts.

Target audience: The timing of a social media campaign should be based on the target audience. For example, if the target audience is young professionals, it may be more effective to post during weekday business hours when they are likely to be checking their social media accounts.

Timing

Industry and competition: The timing of a social media campaign should also be considered in the context of the industry and competition. For example, if a company is launching a new product in a crowded market, it may be necessary to post at a time when competitors are less active in order to stand out.

Platform algorithms: Each social media platform has its own algorithms that determine when and how often a post will be shown to users. It's important to consider these algorithms when determining the timing for a social media campaign. For example, posts on Instagram are more likely to be shown to users if they are posted when the user is most active on the platform.

Holidays and special events: The timing of a social media campaign should also be considered in relation to holidays and special events. For example, a campaign related to a holiday or special event may be more effective if it is launched in the weeks leading up to the event.

Use scheduling tools: There are many tools available that allow businesses to schedule social media posts in advance. This can be especially useful for businesses with a large social media presence or for campaigns that require a consistent posting schedule.

Consider time zones: If a business has a global audience, it's important to consider time zones when determining the timing for a social media campaign. This may involve posting at different times to reach different parts of the world..

Repurposing Content

Repurposing content is the practice of adapting or modifying existing content for use in new contexts or formats. This can be an effective strategy for businesses looking to get the most value out of their content marketing efforts.

Why repurposing content is important for businesses:

Saves time and resources: Repurposing content allows businesses to get more value out of their existing content marketing efforts. This can save time and resources that would otherwise be spent creating new content from scratch.

Reaches new audiences: Repurposing content can help businesses to reach new audiences by adapting content for different formats or platforms. For example, a blog post may be more effective as a video or podcast, which can reach new audiences.

Increases engagement: Repurposing content can help businesses to increase engagement by providing fresh, relevant content to their audience. This can be especially important for businesses with a large social media presence, where it's important to consistently post engaging content.

Improves SEO: Repurposing content can also help businesses to improve their SEO efforts by creating additional pages on their website and providing more opportunities to include relevant keywords and internal and external links.

Repurposing Content

Increases brand awareness: Repurposing content can help businesses to increase their brand awareness by sharing their content on different platforms and in different formats. This can help to expose the business to new audiences and establish the business as an authority in their industry.

Builds thought leadership: By consistently creating and sharing high-quality content, businesses can establish themselves as thought leaders in their industry. Repurposing content allows businesses to share their expertise with a wider audience and establish themselves as go-to sources for information and insights.

Improves customer loyalty: Repurposing content can also help businesses to improve customer loyalty by providing valuable resources and insights to their audience. By consistently creating and sharing valuable content, businesses can build strong relationships with their customers and keep them coming back for more.

Increases conversions: By repurposing content and adapting it to different formats and platforms, businesses can increase their chances of converting visitors into customers. By providing a variety of content formats, businesses can appeal to a wider audience and increase the chances of converting visitors into customers.

Repurposing Content

How you can effectively repurposing content?

Identify the content that is worth repurposing: Not all content is worth repurposing. Start by identifying the content that has performed well in the past, or that has the potential to reach a wider audience in a new format.

Determine the goals of the repurposed content: Before repurposing content, it's important to determine the goals of the new content. For example, the goal may be to reach a new audience, to drive more traffic to the website, or to increase engagement on social media.

Adapt the content to the new format: When repurposing content, it's important to adapt it to the new format. This may involve changing the length of the content, adding or removing certain sections, or including new images or graphics.

Promote the repurposed content: Once the content has been repurposed, it's important to promote it effectively. This may involve sharing the content on social media, email marketing, or other channels.

Mix up the format: One way to effectively repurpose content is to mix up the format. For example, a blog post can be turned into a video, a podcast, or an infographic. This allows businesses to reach new audiences and keep their content fresh and engaging.

Repurposing Content

Use a content calendar: A content calendar can be a useful tool for planning and scheduling the repurposing of content. By mapping out the content that will be repurposed and when it will be published, businesses can ensure that their content strategy is consistent and effective.

Keep SEO in mind: When repurposing content, it's important to keep SEO in mind. This includes optimizing the content for relevant keywords, using appropriate tags and formatting, and including internal and external links as appropriate.

Analyze performance: Regularly analyze the performance of repurposed content to see which formats and strategies are most effective. Use this information to adjust future content repurposing efforts as needed.

Create a series: One way to repurpose content is to create a series of related posts or videos. For example, a business could take a series of blog posts on a particular topic and turn them into a video series or podcast series.

Repurpose content for different audiences: Another way to repurpose content is to adapt it for different audiences. For example, a business could take a blog post and create a version for a more general audience, as well as a version for a more specific niche.

Create a quiz or poll: A quiz or poll is a fun and engaging way to repurpose content. For example, a business could take a blog post on a particular topic and create a quiz or poll based on the information in the post.

Repurposing Content

Use social media to share snippets: Social media platforms are a great place to share snippets of content, such as quotes or statistics, from longer pieces of content. This can help to drive traffic back to the original content and increase engagement.

Create a resource page: A resource page is a dedicated page on a website that includes a collection of valuable resources on a particular topic. This could include blog posts, videos, podcasts, or other types of content. By repurposing content and organizing it on a resource page, businesses can make it easier for users to find and consume their content.

Host a webinar or live event: Webinars and live events are a great way to repurpose content and engage with an audience in real-time. For example, a business could take a series of blog posts on a particular topic and use them as the basis for a webinar or live event.

Turn content into a presentation: Another way to repurpose content is to turn it into a presentation. This could be a slide deck or a more traditional presentation format. This can be a great way to share content with a larger audience, such as at a conference or event.

Use content to create a lead magnet: A lead magnet is a valuable resource that is offered in exchange for a user's contact information. By repurposing content and turning it into a lead magnet, businesses can capture leads and grow their email list.

A/B Testing

A/B testing, also known as split testing, is a method used to compare two versions of a website or marketing campaign to determine which version is more effective. A/B testing allows businesses to make informed decisions about their marketing efforts by measuring the performance of different variations of their content or campaigns.

A/B testing can be used to optimize a variety of marketing efforts, including website design, email marketing campaigns, and social media advertising. By regularly conducting A/B testing, businesses can continuously improve their marketing efforts and achieve better results.

There are a few key steps to follow when conducting A/B testing:

Identify the goal of the test: The first step in A/B testing is to identify the goal of the test. This could be to increase conversions, improve website performance, or any other metric that the business wants to optimize.

Select the element to test: Once the goal of the test has been identified, the next step is to select the element to test. This could be the layout of a landing page, the color of a button, or the subject line of an email.

Create the variations: The next step is to create the variations that will be tested. For example, if the element being tested is the layout of a landing page, the business may create two different versions of the page with different layouts.

A/B Testing

Run the test: Once the variations have been created, the test can be run. This involves sending equal amounts of traffic to each variation and measuring the performance of each one.

Test one element at a time: It's important to only test one element at a time when conducting A/B testing. This will ensure that the results of the test can be attributed to a specific change, rather than being influenced by multiple variables.

Use a large sample size: A/B testing requires a large sample size in order to be effective. This is because the results of the test are based on statistical analysis, and a larger sample size will provide more accurate results.

Monitor the results over time: It's important to monitor the results of A/B testing over time to ensure that the results are consistent. This will help to ensure that the results are not a fluke and can be relied upon when making decisions about marketing efforts.

Keep an open mind: A/B testing can sometimes produce unexpected results, so it's important to keep an open mind and be willing to consider changes that may not have been originally planned.

Use tools to automate the process: There are a variety of tools available that can automate the process of A/B testing. These tools can help businesses to easily create and run tests, as well as analyze the results.

A/B Testing

Test multiple variations: While it's important to only test one element at a time, it's also a good idea to test multiple variations of that element. For example, if the element being tested is the color of a button, the business may want to test several different colors to determine which one is the most effective.

Test on different devices: It's important to test on different devices, as the results of a test may vary based on the device being used. For example, a website that performs well on desktop may not perform as well on mobile.

Test on different audience segments: A/B testing can also be used to test different audience segments to determine which variations are most effective for specific groups of users.

Analyze the results: The final step in A/B testing is to analyze the results and determine which variation performed the best. This can be done using a variety of tools, such as Google Analytics.

A/B Testing

Top 20 A/B testing tools that businesses can use to optimize their marketing efforts:

Google Optimize: A free tool from Google that allows businesses to test different variations of their website and measure the results.

Optimizely: A platform that allows businesses to conduct A/B testing on their website and mobile apps.

Unbounce: A platform that allows businesses to create and test landing pages to optimize conversions.

Crazy Egg: A tool that provides heatmaps and scroll maps to help businesses understand how users interact with their website.

VWO: A platform that allows businesses to conduct A/B testing on their website and mobile apps.

Leadpages: A platform that allows businesses to create and test landing pages to optimize conversions.

Mixpanel: A tool that provides analytics and A/B testing capabilities for mobile apps.

Convert: A platform that allows businesses to conduct A/B testing on their website and mobile apps.

Landingi: A platform that allows businesses to create and test landing pages to optimize conversions.

A/B Testing

ConvertFlow: A tool that allows businesses to create and test landing pages to optimize conversions.

Hootsuite Ads: A platform that allows businesses to conduct A/B testing on their social media advertising campaigns.

AdEspresso: A tool that allows businesses to conduct A/B testing on their Facebook and Instagram advertising campaigns.

Buffer: A tool that allows businesses to schedule and analyze their social media posts, as well as conduct A/B testing on their Instagram advertising campaigns.

Sprout Social: A platform that provides social media management and analytics tools, including the ability to conduct A/B testing on social media advertising campaigns.

SocialFlow: A tool that allows businesses to optimize the timing and targeting of their social media posts, as well as conduct A/B testing on their social media advertising campaigns.

Zoho Social: A platform that provides social media management and analytics tools, including the ability to conduct A/B testing on social media advertising campaigns.

CoSchedule Headline Analyzer: A tool that helps businesses to optimize their headlines and subject lines by conducting A/B testing.

A/B Testing

SubjectLine: A tool that helps businesses to optimize their email subject lines by conducting A/B testing.

Mailchimp: A platform that provides email marketing tools, including the ability to conduct A/B testing on email campaigns.

AWeber: A platform that provides email marketing tools, including the ability to conduct A/B testing on email campaigns.

User-Generated Content

User-generated content (UGC) is any form of content that is created and shared by users, rather than the company or brand. This can include reviews, comments, ratings, photos, and videos.

UGC can be an effective marketing tool for businesses, as it helps to build trust and credibility with consumers. When users see other people using and enjoying a product or service, it can be more persuasive than traditional marketing messages.

User-generated content (UGC) is important for a number of reasons:

It's authentic: One of the biggest benefits of UGC is that it is authentic. When users create and share content about a product or service, it is coming from a real person who has actually used the product. This authenticity can be more persuasive than traditional marketing messages.

It's social proof: UGC can also act as social proof, showing that other people are using and enjoying a product or service. When users see other people using a product, it can increase their confidence in the product and make them more likely to make a purchase.

It can drive engagement: UGC can also help to drive engagement with a brand. When users create and share content, it can help to build a community around a brand and encourage more people to engage with the brand.

User-Generated Content

It's cost-effective: Using UGC in marketing campaigns can also be a cost-effective way to promote a product or service. Rather than creating all of the content in-house, businesses can leverage the content that users are already creating and sharing.

It helps to build trust and credibility: By encouraging customers to create and share content, and featuring that content in marketing campaigns, businesses can effectively build trust and credibility with consumers. When users see other people using and enjoying a product or service, it can be more persuasive than traditional marketing messages.

There are a few key ways that businesses can use UGC to their advantage:

Encourage customers to leave reviews: Encouraging customers to leave reviews on a company's website or social media pages can help to build trust and credibility with potential customers.

Use UGC in marketing campaigns: Featuring user-generated content in marketing campaigns can help to show the real-life use of a product or service, which can be more persuasive than traditional marketing messages.

Run UGC contests: Running contests that encourage users to create and share content can help to drive engagement and build a community around a brand.

User-Generated Content

Choose the right platforms: To effectively leverage UGC, it's important for businesses to choose the right platforms. For example, if a business sells a physical product, then using platforms like Instagram or Pinterest, where users share photos and videos of products, may be more effective. On the other hand, if a business sells a service, then using platforms like Yelp or Trustpilot, where users leave reviews, may be more effective.

Foster a community: To encourage users to create and share content, it's important for businesses to foster a community around their brand. This can be done through social media, forums, or other online platforms where users can connect and share their experiences with a product or service.

Monitor and respond to UGC: It's also important for businesses to monitor and respond to UGC. This can help to build trust and credibility with consumers, and also give businesses the opportunity to address any negative feedback or issues that may arise.

Social Media Advertising

Social media advertising refers to the use of social media platforms to promote a product or service. This can be done through sponsored posts, sponsored hashtags, or paid advertising on platforms like Facebook, Instagram, Twitter, TikTok, YouTube, Google, Pinterest and LinkedIn.

Social media advertising allows businesses to reach and engage with their target audience on platforms where they are already active and engaged. By using targeted advertising, businesses can reach specific audiences based on factors like age, location, interests, and behaviors, and track the performance of their ads in real-time using analytics tools.

There are a few key benefits to using social media advertising:

Targeted advertising: Social media platforms offer a range of targeting options, allowing businesses to reach specific audiences based on factors like age, location, interests, and behaviors. This can help businesses to get their message in front of the right people at the right time.

Quick results: Social media advertising can also deliver quick results. Unlike traditional forms of advertising, which can take weeks or even months to see results, social media advertising can deliver results in just a few hours or days.

Social Media Advertising

Reach and engage with a targeted audience: Social media advertising allows businesses to reach and engage with their target audience on platforms where they are already active and engaged. By using targeted advertising, businesses can reach specific audiences based on factors like age, location, interests, and behaviors.

Measurable results: Most social media platforms offer robust analytics tools, allowing businesses to track the performance of their ads and see how they are performing in real-time. This can help businesses to optimize their campaigns and get the best return on investment.

Cost-effective: Social media advertising can be an affordable way to reach a large audience. Most platforms offer flexible budget options, allowing businesses to choose how much they want to spend and set their own budget limits.

Integration with other marketing efforts: Social media advertising can also be integrated with other marketing efforts, such as email marketing, content marketing, and influencer marketing, to create a holistic marketing strategy.

Increased brand awareness: Social media advertising can help to increase brand awareness by getting a business's message in front of a large audience. When people see a business's ads on social media, they may become more aware of the business and its products or services.

Social Media Advertising

Improved customer engagement: Social media advertising can also help businesses to improve customer engagement. By creating ads that are relevant, interesting, and valuable to their target audience, businesses can encourage more people to engage with their brand.

Greater customer loyalty: Social media advertising can also help businesses to build customer loyalty. By regularly promoting products or services and engaging with customers on social media, businesses can create a sense of community and loyalty among their customers.

Increased website traffic and sales: Ultimately, the goal of social media advertising is often to drive website traffic and increase sales. By creating ads that are targeted and relevant to their target audience, businesses can effectively drive traffic to their website and increase sales.

Choosing the right platform: It's important for businesses to choose the right social media platform for their advertising efforts. Different platforms have different target audiences and offer different ad formats and targeting options. For example, LinkedIn is a good choice for B2B companies, while Facebook is more suitable for B2C companies.

Creating compelling ad copy and visuals: To be effective, social media ads need to grab people's attention and convince them to take action. This means creating compelling ad copy that clearly communicates the value of a product or service, and using visually appealing graphics and images.

Social Media Advertising

Testing and optimization: It's also important for businesses to test and optimize their social media ads to get the best results. This can involve A/B testing different ad versions to see which performs best, and using analytics tools to track the performance of ads and identify areas for improvement.

Staying up to date with platform changes: Finally, it's important for businesses to stay up to date with changes to social media platforms, as these can impact the effectiveness of their advertising efforts. For example, Facebook and Instagram regularly update their algorithms, which can affect the reach and engagement of ads.

Overall, social media advertising is a powerful tool for businesses looking to reach and engage with their target audience, increase brand awareness, improve customer engagement, build customer loyalty, and drive website traffic and sales. By choosing the right platform, creating compelling ad copy and visuals, testing and optimizing ads, and staying up to date with platform changes, businesses can effectively leverage the power of social media advertising to achieve their marketing goals.

Social Media Advertising

Top 10 social media advertising platforms:

Facebook Ads: Facebook's advertising platform allows businesses to create and target ads to specific audiences based on demographics, interests, and behaviors.

Instagram Ads: Instagram's advertising platform, which is owned by Facebook, allows businesses to create and target ads to specific audiences on the photo-sharing platform.

LinkedIn Ads: LinkedIn's advertising platform allows businesses to create and target ads to specific audiences on the professional networking site.

Twitter Ads: Twitter's advertising platform allows businesses to create and target ads to specific audiences on the microblogging site.

Pinterest Ads: Pinterest's advertising platform allows businesses to create and target ads to specific audiences on the visual discovery platform.

Google Ads: Google's advertising platform allows businesses to create and target ads to specific audiences across the Google network, including search, display, and video ads.

Hootsuite Ads: Hootsuite's advertising platform allows businesses to create and target ads to specific audiences on social media platforms, including Facebook, Instagram, LinkedIn, and Twitter.

Social Media Advertising

AdRoll: AdRoll is a tool that allows businesses to create and target ads to specific audiences across multiple social media platforms, including Facebook, Instagram, LinkedIn, and Twitter.

AdWords: AdWords is Google's advertising platform, which allows businesses to create and target ads to specific audiences on the Google network.

HubSpot: HubSpot is a marketing, sales, and customer service platform that includes social media management and advertising tools.

Influencer Marketing

Influencer marketing is a type of marketing that involves working with individuals who have a large following or influence on social media or in a specific industry. These individuals, called "influencers," are often seen as thought leaders or experts in their field and are able to reach and influence a large audience through their social media platforms, blogs, or other channels.

Businesses often work with influencers to promote their products or services to their followers. This can be done through sponsored posts, sponsored giveaways, or other forms of sponsored content. Influencer marketing can be an effective way for businesses to reach a targeted audience, as influencers often have a high level of engagement and credibility with their followers.

Influencer marketing can be an effective way for businesses to reach a targeted audience and build brand awareness.

Some of the benefits of influencer marketing include:

Reach: Influencers often have a large and engaged following, which can be a valuable asset for businesses looking to reach a specific audience.

Trust: Influencers are often seen as experts or thought leaders in their field, and their followers often trust their recommendations. This can be particularly valuable for businesses looking to build trust and credibility with potential customers.

Influencer Marketing

Targeting: Influencer marketing allows businesses to target a specific audience based on the influencer's niche or expertise.

Engagement: Influencers often have high levels of engagement with their followers, which can lead to increased brand awareness and sales.

Cost-effectiveness: Influencer marketing can be a cost-effective way for businesses to reach a targeted audience, especially compared to traditional advertising methods.

Increased sales: Influencer marketing can drive sales by encouraging followers to purchase products or services recommended by the influencer.

There are several key considerations for businesses looking to incorporate influencer marketing into their overall marketing strategy. Some things to consider include:

Setting clear goals: It's important to have clear goals in mind when working with influencers. This could include increasing brand awareness, driving sales, or building trust and credibility with potential customers.

Identifying the right influencers: Not all influencers are created equal, and it's important to carefully research and select the right influencers to work with based on their niche, audience, and level of engagement.

Influencer Marketing

Developing a strategy: It's important to have a clear plan in place for how you will work with influencers and what type of content you will create together. This could include sponsored posts, sponsored giveaways, or other forms of sponsored content.

Tracking results: It's important to track the results of your influencer marketing campaigns to understand what's working and what's not. This could include metrics such as engagement, reach, and sales.

Building relationships: Influencer marketing is about building relationships with influencers and their followers. It's important to be authentic and transparent, and to focus on building long-term partnerships rather than one-off campaigns.

Niche: It's important to choose influencers who are aligned with your brand and target audience. This will help ensure that the influencer's followers are interested in your products or services.

Audience size and engagement: Influencers with a large following may not always be the best choice, as they may not have as high levels of engagement with their followers. It's important to look at both the size of an influencer's audience and the level of engagement they have with their followers.

Authenticity: It's important to choose influencers who are authentic and genuine, as their followers will be more likely to trust their recommendations.

Influencer Marketing

Relevance: It's important to choose influencers who are relevant to your brand and target audience. This will help ensure that the influencer's followers are interested in your products or services.

Transparency: It's important to choose influencers who are transparent about any sponsored content or partnerships. This will help ensure that their followers trust their recommendations.

Develop a clear plan: It's important to have a clear plan in place for how you will work with influencers and what type of content you will create together. This could include sponsored posts, sponsored giveaways, or other forms of sponsored content.

Communicate openly and frequently: It's important to have open and frequent communication with influencers to ensure that everyone is on the same page and that any questions or concerns are addressed promptly.

Offer support and resources: Provide influencers with any support or resources they need to effectively promote your brand and products. This could include access to product samples, images, or other materials.

Track results and adjust as needed: It's important to track the results of your influencer marketing campaigns and adjust your strategy as needed based on what's working and what's not.

Influencer Marketing

How to find the right influencer?

Research: Research popular social media platforms and hashtags related to your industry to find influencers who are active in your niche.

Use influencer marketing platforms: There are several platforms, such as Upfluence, Aspire IQ, and BrandSnob, that can help businesses find influencers to work with. These platforms often allow businesses to search for influencers based on factors such as location, audience size, and content focus.

Look to your own followers: Consider reaching out to followers who are already engaged with your brand to see if they would be interested in collaborating on a social media marketing campaign.

Use social media listening tools: Social media listening tools, such as Hootsuite or Mention, can help businesses track mentions of their brand and identify potential influencers who are interested in their products or services.

Audience size: It's important to consider the size of an influencer's audience, as this will impact the reach of your campaign.

Engagement: Look for influencers who have high levels of engagement, as this indicates that their followers are actively interested in their content and are more likely to take action based on their recommendations.

Influencer Marketing

Relevance: Choose influencers who are relevant to your brand and industry, as their followers are more likely to be interested in your products or services.

Authenticity: Look for influencers who are authentic and genuine, as this will help build trust with their followers and increase the effectiveness of your campaign.

Cost: Consider the cost of working with an influencer, as this will impact your budget and overall campaign strategy.

Social Media Contests and Giveaways

Social media contests and giveaways are promotional campaigns that businesses can use to engage with their followers and drive traffic to their website or social media pages. These campaigns can take many forms, such as photo contests, trivia quizzes, or sweepstakes.

Contests and giveaways can be a powerful marketing tool for businesses, as they can help to increase brand awareness, drive traffic and engagement, and collect valuable customer data. However, it's important to carefully plan and execute these campaigns to ensure they are successful.

Benefits to using social media contests and giveaways

Increased engagement: Contests and giveaways can be a great way to encourage followers to interact with your brand, such as by sharing a post or commenting on a photo.

Increased brand awareness: Contests and giveaways can help to increase the visibility of your brand, as followers will share and promote your campaign with their own followers.

Customer data collection: Contests and giveaways can be a valuable source of customer data, as participants may be required to provide their contact information or answer survey questions.

Increased traffic and sales: Contests and giveaways can drive traffic to your website or social media pages, which can potentially lead to increased sales.

Social Media Contests and Giveaways

Improved customer relationships: Contests and giveaways can help to strengthen relationships with customers and build brand loyalty.

To run a successful social media contest or giveaway, businesses should:

Set clear goals and objectives: Determine what you want to achieve with your campaign, such as increasing brand awareness or driving sales.

Choose the right platform: Select the social media platform that is most appropriate for your target audience and campaign goals.

Develop a compelling offer: Create an offer that will be appealing to your target audience and aligns with your campaign goals.

Promote your contest or giveaway: Use a variety of tactics, such as social media posts, email marketing, and paid advertising, to promote your contest or giveaway.

Follow the rules: Make sure you are following all relevant rules and regulations, such as those related to sweepstakes and contests.

Social Media Contests and Giveaways

There are also a few key considerations to keep in mind when running social media contests and giveaways:

Legal and regulatory compliance: Make sure you are following all relevant laws and regulations, such as those related to sweepstakes and contests. This includes getting proper consent from participants and disclosing any rules or restrictions.

Targeting the right audience: Choose a prize or theme that will be appealing to your target audience and aligns with your marketing goals.

Setting clear rules and guidelines: Clearly outline the rules and guidelines for your contest or giveaway, including how to enter, how winners will be chosen, and any eligibility requirements.

By following these considerations, businesses can run successful social media contests and giveaways that achieve their marketing goals.

Customer Service

Customer service refers to the actions and processes a company takes to address and resolve the needs and concerns of its customers. This can include providing product or service support, answering customer questions, handling complaints or issues, and offering assistance with orders or other requests.

Effective customer service is essential for businesses, as it can help to build customer loyalty, improve the customer experience, and drive sales. It is also important for businesses to have a clear customer service strategy in place, which outlines the processes and resources that will be used to address customer needs and concerns.

There are a variety of ways that businesses can provide customer service, including:

Phone: Many businesses offer phone support for customers, allowing them to call and speak with a representative to get help or ask questions.

Email: Many businesses offer email support, allowing customers to send inquiries or complaints to a designated email address.

Chat: Some businesses offer chat support, which allows customers to communicate with a representative in real-time through a chat window on the company's website.

Social media: Many businesses use social media platforms, such as Facebook and Twitter, to communicate with customers and address their concerns.

Customer Service

There are several key factors that contribute to effective customer service:

Responsiveness: Customers expect timely responses to their inquiries or complaints, so it is important for businesses to have a system in place to respond to customer needs in a timely manner.

Empathy: Showing empathy and understanding towards customers can go a long way in building trust and improving the customer experience. This includes actively listening to the customer's concerns and trying to find solutions that meet their needs.

Knowledge: Customer service representatives should have a thorough understanding of the company's products or services, as well as any policies or procedures related to customer support. This can help them to more effectively address customer needs and concerns.

Professionalism: Maintaining a professional and courteous demeanor is essential for building trust and credibility with customers. This includes using appropriate language, staying calm and patient, and following through on any commitments made to the customer.

Flexibility: Being able to adapt to the changing needs and concerns of customers is important for providing effective customer service. This may involve offering alternative solutions or being willing to go the extra mile to meet customer needs.

Customer Service

Use a variety of channels: Different customers may prefer different channels for communicating with a business, so it is important to offer a range of options. This may include phone, email, chat, social media, or in-person support.

Train employees: Proper training is essential for ensuring that customer service representatives have the knowledge and skills necessary to effectively address customer needs. This may include training on company policies and procedures, as well as customer service best practices.

Monitor and measure customer satisfaction: It is important for businesses to regularly monitor and measure customer satisfaction to ensure that they are meeting customer needs and identifying areas for improvement. This can be done through surveys, focus groups, or other methods.

Use technology to improve efficiency: There are a variety of tools and technologies that can help businesses to more efficiently manage customer service, such as customer relationship management (CRM) systems and chatbots.

Chatbots are automated programs that use artificial intelligence (AI) to communicate with users through messaging platforms, such as chat windows on websites or messaging apps. They can be used to provide customer service by answering common questions, directing users to relevant information or resources, and helping to resolve issues or problems.

Customer Service

Here are a few ways that chatbots can be used in social media marketing customer service:

Responding to customer inquiries: Chatbots can be programmed to answer common customer questions, such as product or service inquiries, delivery or shipping questions, or account-related inquiries.

Providing personalized recommendations: Chatbots can use customer data to provide personalized product or service recommendations based on a user's interests or previous purchases.

Resolving issues or problems: Chatbots can be programmed to help customers resolve issues or problems they are experiencing, such as trouble placing an order or accessing an account.

Gathering customer feedback: Chatbots can be used to gather customer feedback through surveys or other methods, which can help businesses to improve their products or services.

Customer Service

Popular Customer Relationship Management (CRM) tools:

Salesforce: A comprehensive CRM platform that includes sales, marketing, and customer service tools.

HubSpot: A CRM platform that includes sales, marketing, and customer service tools, as well as analytics and reporting capabilities.

Zoho: A CRM platform that includes sales, marketing, and customer service tools, as well as project management and collaboration features.

Freshworks: A CRM platform that includes sales, marketing, and customer service tools, as well as tools for managing customer support tickets and live chats.

Microsoft Dynamics: A CRM platform that includes sales, marketing, and customer service tools, as well as integration with other Microsoft products.

Infusionsoft: A CRM platform that includes sales, marketing, and customer service tools, as well as tools for automating business processes.

Pipedrive: A CRM platform specifically designed for sales teams, with features for managing sales pipelines and tracking deals.

SugarCRM: A CRM platform that includes sales, marketing, and customer service tools, as well as tools for managing customer data and analytics.

Customer Service

Insightly: A CRM platform that includes sales, marketing, and customer service tools, as well as tools for managing projects and tasks.

Copper: A CRM platform specifically designed for small businesses, with features for managing customer relationships and sales pipelines.

Agile CRM: A CRM platform that includes sales, marketing, and customer service tools, as well as tools for automating business processes and managing projects.

Bitrix24: A CRM platform that includes sales, marketing, and customer service tools, as well as tools for managing tasks and projects, and for collaboration within teams.

Act!: A CRM platform that includes sales, marketing, and customer service tools, as well as tools for managing customer data and analytics.

Salesforce Pardot: A CRM platform specifically designed for B2B marketing, with features for lead generation, nurturing, and scoring.

Zendesk: A CRM platform that includes customer service tools, such as a help desk and live chat, as well as tools for managing customer data and analytics.

Social Media Analytics

Social media analytics refers to the process of collecting, measuring, and analyzing data from social media platforms. This data can be used to understand the performance and effectiveness of social media marketing efforts, as well as to gain insights into the preferences, behaviors, and sentiments of social media users.

There are many different tools and techniques that businesses can use to conduct social media analytics, including native analytics tools provided by social media platforms, third-party analytics tools, and custom analytics solutions.

By analyzing data from social media platforms, businesses can:

Measure the engagement and reach of their content: Social media analytics tools can help businesses understand how well their content is performing in terms of likes, comments, shares, and other forms of engagement. This can help businesses identify which types of content are most effective at resonating with their audience and which types may not be performing as well.

Understand their audience: Social media analytics tools can provide businesses with insights into the demographics, interests, and behaviors of their audience. This can help businesses tailor their marketing efforts to better target their desired audience and create more relevant and effective content.

Social Media Analytics

Track the impact of their efforts: Social media analytics tools can help businesses track the impact of their social media marketing efforts over time. For example, businesses can use analytics tools to track the number of visits to their website or online store from social media platforms, as well as the number of leads or sales generated through social media.

Identify trends and opportunities: By analyzing data from social media platforms, businesses can identify trends and patterns in their audience's behavior and preferences. This can help businesses identify new opportunities for engagement and growth on social media.

Improve customer service: Social media analytics tools can also be used to track and analyze customer feedback and inquiries on social media platforms. This can help businesses identify areas for improvement in their customer service efforts and respond to customer needs more effectively.

Some common types of data that may analyze include:

Engagement metrics: This includes metrics such as likes, comments, and shares, which can help businesses understand how well their content is resonating with their audience.

Audience demographics: This includes data such as age, gender, location, and interests, which can help businesses understand who their audience is and what they care about.

Social Media Analytics

Traffic and referrals: This includes data on the number of visits to a business's website or online store from social media platforms, as well as data on which social media platforms are driving the most traffic.

Sentiment analysis: This involves using natural language processing and machine learning techniques to analyze the tone and sentiment of social media posts, which can help businesses understand how their brand is perceived on social media.

Competitive analysis: This involves analyzing data from competitors' social media accounts, which can help businesses understand how their own performance compares to that of their competitors.

Reach: This measures the number of people who see a particular social media post or message.

Click-through rate (CTR): This measures the number of clicks on a link in a social media post or message, divided by the number of times the post or message was seen.

Conversion rate: This measures the number of people who take a desired action (such as making a purchase or signing up for a newsletter) after clicking on a social media link.

Customer acquisition cost (CAC): This measures the cost of acquiring a new customer through social media marketing efforts.

Social Media Analytics

Customer lifetime value (CLV): This measures the total value of a customer to a business over the lifetime of their relationship.

ROI: This measures the return on investment from social media marketing efforts.

Influencer score: This measures the influence of a particular individual or group on social media.

Hashtag performance: This measures the performance of specific hashtags on social media, including reach, engagement, and sentiment.

Audience growth: This measures the rate at which a business' social media audience is growing.

Content performance: This measures the performance of specific pieces of content on social media, including reach, engagement, and conversion rate.

Social media sales: This measures the total value of sales generated through social media marketing efforts.

Social media ad spend: This measures the total amount of money spent on social media advertising.

Social media lead generation: This measures the number of leads generated through social media marketing efforts.

Social Media Analytics

Popular social media analytics tools:

Hootsuite: A social media management platform that includes analytics tools for measuring the reach and engagement of social media content, tracking website traffic from social media, and identifying trends and opportunities.

Google Analytics: A web analytics tool that can be used to track website traffic from social media platforms, as well as to analyze the behavior of website visitors.

Sprout Social: A social media management and analytics platform that includes tools for measuring engagement, tracking website traffic from social media, and analyzing audience demographics.

Brand24: A social media monitoring and analytics tool that helps businesses track mentions of their brand and analyze sentiment on social media.

Socialbakers: A social media analytics and marketing platform that includes tools for measuring engagement, tracking website traffic from social media, and analyzing audience demographics.

Buffer: A social media management and analytics platform that includes tools for measuring engagement and analyzing audience demographics.

Klout: A social media analytics tool that measures the online influence of individuals and brands by analyzing social media data.

Social Media Analytics

Keyhole: A social media analytics tool that helps businesses track hashtags, keywords, and URLs on social media platforms and analyze the reach and engagement of their content.

Simply Measured: A social media analytics tool that includes tools for measuring engagement, tracking website traffic from social media, and analyzing audience demographics.

SocialFlow: A social media analytics and optimization platform that helps businesses optimize the timing and targeting of their social media posts.

Union Metrics: A social media analytics tool that helps businesses track the performance and reach of their social media content, as well as analyze audience demographics and sentiment.

Agorapulse: A social media management and analytics platform that includes tools for measuring engagement, tracking website traffic from social media, and analyzing audience demographics.

Digimind: A social media monitoring and analytics tool that helps businesses track mentions of their brand and analyze sentiment on social media.

Followerwonk: A social media analytics tool that helps businesses analyze their Twitter followers, as well as compare their social media performance to that of their competitors.

Social Media Analytics

Mention: A social media monitoring and analytics tool that helps businesses track mentions of their brand and analyze sentiment on social media.

NetBase: A social media analytics tool that helps businesses track and analyze social media conversations, as well as measure the sentiment of those conversations.

Meltwater: A social media monitoring and analytics tool that helps businesses track mentions of their brand and analyze sentiment on social media.

Syfe: A social media analytics tool that helps businesses track the performance and reach of their social media content, as well as analyze audience demographics and sentiment.

TweetDeck: A social media management and analytics platform that includes tools for measuring engagement and analyzing audience demographics.

Social Media Monitoring

Social media monitoring refers to the process of tracking and analyzing online conversations and mentions of a brand or topic on social media platforms. It involves using specialized tools or software to track and collect data from social media channels, and then analyzing that data to gain insights about the brand's performance, audience demographics, sentiment, and more.

Social media monitoring helps businesses and organizations to understand how their brand is perceived online, identify trends and insights that can inform marketing and communication strategies, and measure the impact of their social media efforts. It can also help to identify potential customer service issues and manage online reputation.

Some of the key features of social media monitoring tools include the ability to track specific keywords or hashtags, monitor social media accounts and profiles, analyze sentiment and emotions, and visualize data and insights through reports and dashboards.

There are several benefits to using social media monitoring:

Identify trends and insights: Social media monitoring can help businesses to identify trends and insights related to their industry, products, or services. This can inform marketing and communication strategies, as well as help businesses to stay up-to-date with industry developments.

Social Media Monitoring

Improve customer service: By monitoring social media channels, businesses can identify and respond to customer service issues in real-time, improving customer satisfaction and loyalty.

Manage online reputation: Social media monitoring can help businesses to identify and address any negative sentiment or comments about their brand on social media, helping to protect and manage their online reputation.

Measure the impact of social media efforts: By tracking and analyzing data from social media channels, businesses can measure the impact of their social media efforts and identify areas for improvement.

Targeted advertising: Social media monitoring can help businesses to identify key influencers and target their advertising efforts towards specific groups or demographics.

Competitive analysis: Social media monitoring can also help businesses to track and compare their social media performance to that of their competitors. This can inform marketing strategies and help businesses to stay ahead of the competition.

Build relationships with customers and influencers: By monitoring social media channels and engaging with customers and influencers, businesses can build relationships and foster a sense of community on social media.

Social Media Monitoring

Monitor brand mentions: Social media monitoring can help businesses to track and analyze brand mentions on social media, helping them to understand how their brand is perceived online.

Identify new business opportunities: By monitoring social media conversations and trends, businesses can identify new business opportunities and target their marketing efforts towards specific groups or demographics.

Stay up-to-date with industry developments: By monitoring social media channels and trends, businesses can stay up-to-date with industry developments and identify opportunities for innovation.

Monitor employee social media activity: Social media monitoring can also help businesses to monitor employee social media activity to ensure that they are representing the company in a positive way.

Monitor social media accounts: Social media monitoring tools can help businesses to monitor their own social media accounts and identify areas for improvement, as well as track the performance of their competitors' social media accounts.

Social Media Automation

Social media automation refers to the use of software or tools to automate various tasks and processes related to social media marketing. This can include scheduling posts in advance, automating responses to comments and messages, or automating the creation of social media ads.

Businesses use social media automation for a variety of reasons, including:

Saves time: One of the main benefits of social media automation is that it allows businesses to save time by automating tasks that would otherwise take up a lot of manual effort.

Increases efficiency: Automation can help businesses streamline their social media marketing efforts and improve their overall efficiency by allowing them to schedule posts, automate responses to comments and messages, and create social media ads in advance.

Improves consistency: Social media automation can help businesses maintain a consistent presence on social media, even when they don't have the time or resources to be active on social media every day.

Expands reach: Automation can help businesses reach a wider audience by targeting specific groups of users or promoting content to specific demographics.

Enhances customer service: Automation can also be used to improve customer service by allowing businesses to automatically respond to customer inquiries or complaints on social media.

Social Media Automation

Increases ROI: By automating certain tasks, businesses can free up time and resources to focus on more high-value activities that can drive better results and a higher return on investment (ROI) from their social media marketing efforts.

Improves targeting: Automation tools allow businesses to target specific groups of users based on demographics, interests, and other factors, which can help them reach the right audience with their content.

Provides insights: Many automation tools also offer analytics and reporting capabilities, which can help businesses understand how their social media marketing efforts are performing and what kind of content is resonating with their audience.

Increases brand awareness: By consistently publishing content and engaging with users on social media, businesses can use automation to increase their visibility and build brand awareness.

Improves data collection: Automation tools can also help businesses collect data on their social media activity, which can be used to inform future marketing efforts and make data-driven decisions.

Enhances social media strategy: By using automation to manage certain aspects of their social media marketing efforts, businesses can create a more comprehensive and effective social media strategy.

Social Media Automation

Set up social media automation for your business:

Identify your goals: The first step in implementing social media automation is to identify your goals. What do you hope to achieve through automation? Do you want to save time, reach more people, improve efficiency, or something else?

Choose the right tools: There are many different automation tools available, so it's important to choose the ones that are right for your business. Consider your goals, budget, and the features that are most important to you.

Set up your accounts: Once you have chosen your automation tools, you will need to set up your accounts and connect them to your social media accounts. This may involve creating profiles, linking accounts, and setting up any necessary integrations.

Create your content: Next, you will need to create the content that you want to publish on social media. This can include text updates, images, videos, and links to other content.

Set up your automation rules: Finally, you will need to set up the automation rules that will determine when and how your content is published. This may include scheduling posts in advance, setting up triggers for certain actions, or creating rules for engaging with users.

Social Media Guidelines

Social media guidelines are an important tool for businesses that want to establish a strong and consistent presence on social media platforms. These guidelines provide a framework for how employees should behave on social media and ensure that the company's message is being communicated effectively.

Some of the benefits of having social media guidelines include:

Consistency: Social media guidelines help to ensure that the tone and messaging used by a business is consistent across all social media platforms. This helps to create a cohesive brand identity and strengthens the company's reputation.

Clarity: Social media guidelines provide clear guidelines for employees on how to behave on social media, including what content is appropriate to share and what is not. This can help prevent any social media mistakes that could damage the company's reputation.

Legal compliance: Social media guidelines can help businesses stay compliant with legal regulations, such as laws related to data privacy and consumer protection.

Improved efficiency: Social media guidelines can help streamline the social media process by providing clear guidelines on how to create and share content. This can save time and resources, allowing businesses to focus on other important tasks.

Social Media Guidelines

Increased engagement: By providing clear guidelines on how to engage with customers and followers on social media, businesses can encourage more interaction and build stronger relationships with their audience.

Risk management: Social media guidelines can help businesses identify and mitigate potential risks related to social media use, such as cyberbullying or online harassment.

Reputation management: By setting clear guidelines for how employees should behave on social media, businesses can help protect their reputation and avoid any negative backlash from inappropriate content or behavior.

Employee engagement: Social media guidelines can help employees feel more confident and empowered to use social media as part of their work, as they have clear guidelines on what is expected of them.

Increased productivity: By providing clear guidelines on how to use social media, businesses can help employees stay focused on their work and avoid any distractions.

Social Media Guidelines

10 steps social media guidelines

Introduction: Provide an overview of the purpose of these guidelines and how they will be used. Explain the importance of social media in the modern business landscape and how it can be used to support the company's goals.

Purpose of social media: Explain the business's goals for using social media and how it fits into the overall marketing and communication strategy. This might include increasing brand awareness, engaging with customers, driving website traffic, or generating leads.

Brand representation: Outline the brand's tone, voice, and messaging on social media, and provide guidelines for maintaining consistency across platforms. This might include guidelines for language, tone, and content, as well as guidelines for using the company's logo and branding elements on social media.

Employee participation: Encourage employee engagement on social media, but outline any limitations or guidelines for employee participation. This might include guidelines for identifying oneself as an employee of the company, guidelines for interacting with customers or followers, and guidelines for sharing company information on personal social media accounts.

Content creation: This might include guidelines for using visuals, such as images and videos, as well as guidelines for creating engaging and informative written content.

Social Media Guidelines

Confidentiality: Remind employees to protect company information and intellectual property on social media. This might include guidelines for handling confidential information, such as financial data, product plans, or internal communications.

Legal compliance: Remind employees to adhere to all laws and regulations when using social media, including those related to advertising, privacy, and data protection. This might include guidelines for disclosing sponsored content or paid partnerships, as well as guidelines for collecting and using customer data.

Crisis management: Provide guidelines for handling negative comments or feedback on social media, as well as guidelines for responding to a crisis situation. This might include guidelines for escalating issues to management and guidelines for working with the company's public relations team.

Interacting with customers: Provide guidelines for interacting with customers on social media. This might include guidelines for responding to customer inquiries and complaints, as well as guidelines for handling negative comments or feedback.

Monitoring and analytics: Provide guidelines for monitoring the company's social media presence and for using analytics tools to measure the effectiveness of social media campaigns. This might include guidelines for tracking metrics such as engagement, reach, and conversions, as well as guidelines for using insights to improve future campaigns.

www.ingramcontent.com/pod-product-compliance
Lightning Source LLC
Chambersburg PA
CBHW050005230526
45465CB00003BB/1276